OBITCHUARY

The Big Hot Book of Death

SPENCER HENRY & MADISON REYES

WITH ALLIE KINGSLEY BAKER

PLUME

PLUME

An imprint of Penguin Random House LLC
penguinrandomhouse.com

Copyright © 2024 by Madison Reyes and Spencer Henry
Penguin Random House supports copyright. Copyright fuels creativity, encourages
diverse voices, promotes free speech, and creates a vibrant culture. Thank you for
buying an authorized edition of this book and for complying with copyright laws
by not reproducing, scanning, or distributing any part of it in any form without
permission. You are supporting writers and allowing Penguin Random House to
continue to publish books for every reader.

PLUME and P colophon are registered trademarks of Penguin Random House LLC.

Illustrations by Lauren Griffin
Obituary on pages 170–171 reprinted with permission from Robert Weide.

LIBRARY OF CONGRESS CATALOGING-IN-PUBLICATION DATA
has been applied for.

ISBN 9780593475287 (hardcover)
ISBN 9780593475294 (ebook)

Printed in the United States of America
1st Printing

BOOK DESIGN BY PATRICE SHERIDAN

THIS ONE GOES OUT TO ALL THE DEAD PEOPLE.

CONTENTS

PART 3

FUCKED

PART 4

TILL DEATH DO US PART
(AND MAYBE NOT EVEN THEN)

INTRODUCTION

Dearest reader,

We're so glad you're here! We can assume a lot of things about you by the fact that you decided to pick up a book subtitled *The Big Hot Book of Death*. Are you big? Hot? Dead? None of these are prerequisites to enjoy the material to follow, we're just curious. In fact, curiosity is how we landed ourselves here in the first place!

We, Spencer Henry and Madison Reyes, sort of fell into the world of the macabre, stemming from a long history of sending each other the most outlandish obituaries we could find. That somehow evolved into a podcast, and then—what do you know—a book! A whole fucking book. We laugh all the time about how we ended up here. Come back with us to 2013 and we'll tell you how it all started. . . .

Spencer had begun dating Madison's *former* best friend and had flown down to Los Angeles for the weekend. It's only fitting that the night we met we went to see *Evil Dead* in a theater. Though we hit it off immediately, it wasn't until years later, in 2018, that we jumped from "friends" to "insep-arable" after the unexpected loss of Spencer's sweet mother,

Laurel. Spencer spent a few weeks away with his family, and upon returning to Los Angeles, we started getting together more frequently, and *more* frequently, and we've spent pretty much every day together since. In order to cope with his grief, Spencer started posting online rants about different cult documentaries and true-crime stories, which led to the next natural progression of starting a true-crime podcast, *Cult Liter*, which launched in October 2018. Someway, somehow it turned into a full-time gig in 2021, and around that same time Spencer was struck with another idea for a new show: *OBITCHUARY*. And he realized that Madison would be the perfect partner.

The conversation went something like this:

SPENCER: Okay, hear me out: it's a new show; it's called
    OBITCHUARY but like O-BITCH-UARY.
MADISON: I love it.
SPENCER: We'll read obituaries—we have so many in our
    texts; I think people will love it like we do. Are you in?
MADISON: Let's fucking do it!

We launched the show on Patreon so that Madison could get her feet wet, and quickly found our episodes getting longer and longer as we started incorporating new sections into each show—our "coffin spinners" as we call them. Each "coffin spinner" since has covered anything and everything from caskets versus coffins, haunted cemeteries, unique cremation methods, the history and cost of obituaries . . . which—yeesh—are those things expensive! In fact, that was one that

Spencer had unfortunately come to know about through personal experience.

When *OBITCHUARY* the podcast started taking off, we had no idea it would end up where we've ended up. A podcast network took a chance on us and gave us the tools and financial stability to take this on full-time, and as we write this we're hot off our 2023 US tour, where we performed live for audiences full of our beloved listeners who have become our best friends. Who knew that our off-color humor and campy anecdotes would lead us to strangers on the street telling us we've helped them cope with loss in their own lives? Or a PO Box with handwritten letters thanking us for helping their loved one with a terminal illness decide they wanted to donate their body to a body farm? It's incredible. It's beautiful. And to us, it's the most fulfilling thing either one of us has ever experienced. Neither of us could've imagined this would be our purpose, but it's looking like that just might be the case.

We're sure some of the funeral industry's finest are rolling their eyes at the thought of two podcasters writing a book: *What the hell do they know?!* And they have every right to feel that way. The truth is, before venturing into the topics we discuss on our weekly podcast, we weren't all that familiar with the ins and outs of the afterlife. But it turns out that it's a morbid curiosity many share with us, and we've loved learning alongside our listeners, now readers, about a topic that's long been hushed up by most of society. Plus, you can't really gatekeep death, right? It's the *one* thing we all gotta do. We promise there's room for everyone! Unless we're talking about cemeteries . . . Those things can sure fill up quick. If you're curious about what happens afterward, don't worry, we've got you covered.

Our goal with *The Big Hot Book of Death* is to take you, reader, through the wild, wonderful, and sometimes terrifying world of obituaries, of course, but it doesn't end there. We've come across so many fascinating death-related topics in our years of research, and, honey, we've got a lot to talk about. We're essentially giving you something horrifying to bring up at the dinner table. Sharing a meal with a pompous mother-in-law? Interrupt her with your newfound knowledge of death erections! Going on a first date? Start a healthy debate of cremation versus burial. If they end up ghosting you, they aren't worth your time! Speaking of ghosts, we've got some stories in here sure to startle even the bravest of readers.

We've laid this book out in a way that you can truly flip to any chapter and learn something new. Our brains personally aren't wired in an ABC, 123, left-to-right type of logic, so fellow ADHDers rejoice, this book is for you!

So what can you expect? A romp through death. You might shed some tears or fall into a fit of laughter—honestly, we hope you experience an entire range of emotions as you flip through *The Big Hot Book of Death*, because, let's face it, that's life! It's fun, it's unpredictable, and sometimes it fucking sucks. So allow us to take your mind off the mundane and into the insane.

PART 1

THE END IS
JUST THE BEGINNING

1

WHAT TO EXPECT WHEN YOU'RE NOT EXPECTING

Well, I'm dead. Now what? Surely this has to be the worst of it, right? Wrong.

When we bow out, our bodies experience a series of changes, think of it like a second puberty, or menopause . . . except a helluva lot hotter, depending on your belief system. Speaking of, the one thing we can all agree on as humans is that we have no definitive answers about what happens when we bite the dust. We might cross over to another plane, become reincarnated, or fade into the abyss; regardless, physically, our bodies are left here on earth to wreak havoc—no, literally, sometimes they *reek*.

Before we get into the physical—let's pause for a second to discuss this not-so-fun fact. Apparently scientists and doctors alike are discovering our brains are thought to continue working for ten minutes or so after we die, meaning our brains may in some way be aware of our death. In 2017 a team of Canadian doctors published a paper in the *Canadian Journal of Neurological Sciences* documenting a case of a terminal patient who had been removed from life support and continued to experience ten minutes of brain activity before officially being considered clinically dead! That's something to think about . . . or not.

Fast-forward from there and we go through a stage referred to as Fresh. Real creative, right? Well, it is accurate. During this stage the muscles relax. This is also called primary flaccidity. Eyelids lose their tension, pupils dilate, and the jaw may or may not fall open. At this point the body's joints and limbs are still flexible. Due to the loss of tension in the muscles, the skin may sag, causing bones to appear to be sticking out a little bit. Yes, baby, show off those collarbones, now is the time. This is also when the tone of the sphincter diminishes and you will likely shit yourself, we hope there's no hot paramedic serving witness.

After the heart stops beating, something called pallor mortis occurs, which causes the body to lose its color, so make sure you spray-tan extra well every day just, you know, *in case*. The body will then start cooling off, going into algor mortis, also known as the death chill, typically declining 1.5 degrees per hour.

Between the second and sixth hour, the blood begins to pool at its lowest points as the heart is no longer pump-pump-pumping away. This is called livor mortis—but, baby, ain't nobody liv-ing here, heh? HEH? This is when the not so

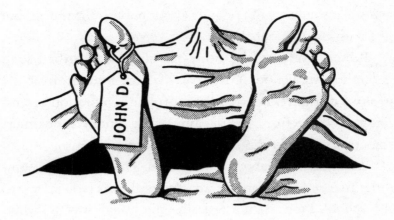

elusive death erection would occur. What is a death erection? So glad you asked. . . .

The long and the short of it is that when someone is hanged, for example, the blood starts to pool in the lower half of the body, which causes an erection once it reaches the penis's erectile tissue. This doesn't always happen every time, it can be blocked by things like blood clots or body position. Basically the body needs to stay vertical in order for the penis to stay erect. And it's not always people who were executed, of course, though it's usually provoked by traumatic deaths.

We read somewhere that sometimes after an act of vengeance against an enemy, people would cut off the erections of the enemy they killed and keep them as trophies, which leads us to . . . the Viktor Wynd Museum of Curiosities, Fine Art & Natural History in Hackney, London, actually had a death erection on display from 2017 to 2018. The boner belonged to a man who had been executed and was titled "The World's Longest Standing Erection." We've seen pictures, and we absolutely will not and cannot publish them here, but just trust us—it's out there.

Boners aside, if the body remains undisturbed long enough (several hours), the parts of the body nearest the ground can develop a reddish-purple discoloration resembling a bruise from the accumulating blood. Embalmers sometimes refer to this as the "postmortem stain."

We've all heard about rigor mortis. That's just the beginning. In case you haven't heard of rigor mortis (you're new to this school, I guess?), it's basically your body's way of saying, *Nobody wake me up.* Your muscles stiffen up, making you about as flexible as a tree.

Maximum stiffness will occur throughout the entire body after roughly twelve hours. After the twelfth hour the body goes into a second flaccidity. This happens over a period of around three days but is very different based on several factors: predominately the climate in which the body resides. The muscles loosen as internal tissue begins to decay, the skin starts to shrink. That's when hair and nails appear to grow, which isn't really true. Yes, unfortunately lying dead in your casket is not the prime opportunity to test out how you'd look with a mustache. Once we pass, our bodies stop producing cells necessary to supply glucose, a necessity for both hair and nail growth. Our skin begins to dry out, and in doing so, it can absolutely make it appear as if our fingernails and hair, particularly facial, is growing, however we're actually just shrinking around it!

To summarize the Fresh stage, we get cold, hard, bruised, and bonered.

Moving along, we have a gnarly phase called Bloat, beginning three to five days after death. This is when microorganisms inside the gut start letting loose and munching down on the tissues. It's during this process that gases excrete, which then makes the torso and the limbs bloat, producing foul odors. This is when the skin starts to slip, oh, and the liquids begin releasing something called "purge fluid" (which, side note: would be a good band name) from the nose and mouth.

Around days eight to ten comes Active Decay. This is the stage where tissues begin to liquefy and the skin begins to darken. The body becomes a bug buffet for flies, maggots, and other creepy-crawlies to lay eggs or feast. Maggots can detect a decaying corpse very early on; the size and development stage of maggots can be used to give a measure of the minimum time since death—super important when it relates to victims of homicide.

Next we have Advanced Decay. Here the remains go through putrefaction, essentially a decomposition disco, where bacteria and enzymes throw a wild party and the tissues and cells break down and liquefy.

The final stage is called Dry, naturally. After bloating, the soft tissue will start to collapse on itself and then dry out and begin to skeletonize. Which, who knew there was a verb for becoming a skeleton—love it! In a temperate climate, it usually requires three weeks to several years for a body to completely decompose into a skeleton, depending on factors such as temperature, humidity, presence of insects, and submergence in a substrate such as water.

Also going on at the same time . . . the smell. We've all heard that death has a super distinct smell . . . one that some say you will never ever forget. Scientists have said odor mortis is an important component of the death process, because in nature it's both an attractant to insects, rodents, reptiles, and mammals, and a repellent to warn of meat spoilage. The very thought of the odor of death is puke inducing, but it does have benefits, especially in the forensic community.

What's crazy about scent is that it doesn't come in waves like our sense of sound or light; instead it comes in molecules that are diffused through the air and reach your nose. Their movement is random, and they just bounce off each other until they fill a space. So the molecules go into your physical body and fit into certain receptors in your brain, and they trigger a smell. It's possible—again, according to scientists— our brain has specific death-smell receptors. Which to us makes sense because we have always heard that the smell of death is recognizable even if you've never smelled it before; it's like an innate sense of *that's something DEAD!* However, smell is pretty subjective to everyone . . . so your death smell and my death smell may smell way different.

It turns out the same chemicals that cause the scent of a decaying body to attract and repulse also contribute to bad breath and the smell and taste in semen. We'll just leave that right there.

For the *Dateline* junkies out there, you're probably familiar with young mother Casey Anthony, who was accused of murdering her two-year-old daughter. There was quite the controversy over whether the judge would allow a sample of air, collected from the trunk of Casey's car, to be presented as evidence of the "smell of death." In Casey's father's testimony, he said that he was concerned about the odor coming from her car. He had smelled that same smell a few years prior, and it was that of a decomposing body. The supervisor from the tow yard who kept her car also testified saying that it smelled "like a dead body." Is the smell a biological response? An innate aversion we as humans have? Or is it something we've learned about through movies and books, where the odor is already in our minds?

People say the scent notes of death have elements of an earthy musk yet they are simply putrid, strong and intense. It's been said that it is difficult to tolerate because of how overpowering and unpleasant it is. Can we just stop here? Yes? Okay, end scene.

So, to summarize—we're dead, decomposed; we stink. Now what? Rewind back to when you were alive. What did you want to do with your body once you were dead? It's a common question with a typically common answer: either cremation or burial. Those are my choices, right? So wrong! Dare we even say . . . dead wrong? Too much? There's a plethora of ways to peace out, starting with but not limited to alkaline hydrolysis (dissolving in water); donating your parts to a body farm; eco-friendly burials, such as being buried in a mushroom suit, which, fun fact, was chosen by actor Luke Perry; cryonics (freezing your whole body—or even just your head!—until science enables us to bring you back to life); and then there's getting turned into a diamond, ink, paint, a firework, a coral reef, or a sculpture. There's even a place that

will preserve your tattoos as art for your loved ones to adorn the walls. Yeah, we've heard a lot of stuff, and that's the one that makes *our* skin crawl. And that's saying a lot. The fascinating and sometimes wild ways people want to go out is one we are experts on.

When it comes to what happens to your body postmortem, you've got options. Lots of 'em. Let's begin with the obvious go-tos before getting into the really weird stuff.

Embalming: This classic choice involves injecting chemicals (like formaldehyde) into the body to slow down decomposition. It's like giving your body a pickling treatment, keeping it looking presentable for viewings and funerals. Taking this to the next level is something called "extreme embalming," which requires preserving the deceased in a very personal and lifelike way. Rather than the traditional presentation of a body reclining in a casket, extreme embalming takes creativity to a whole new level. In this process, corpses are given more of an extra appearance. They look more camera- than coffin-ready. They may be posed in a way that represents their hobbies or other interests. For example, swinging a nine iron, sitting down to afternoon tea, or posing in a fishing boat as if they're about to make a big catch. Embalming doesn't stop the natural decaying of the body, it just slows it down. So in most cases, these sets are meant for display, often at the funeral for friends and family to pay their respects.

Burial: Good ol' underground resting place, whether in a traditional coffin, a biodegradable one, or even a mausoleum. Here your body gets cozy with Mother Earth, but depending on the cemetery, don't get too comfortable! Because it turns out, "rest in peace" sometimes comes with a time limit. For example, in some cemeteries in Greece you are required to rent-a-grave, which would allot you the space for about three years and when your lease is up, you either renew or ya gotta move!

Most American cemeteries promise eternal resting places, but in some countries, that's not a given. And with America being relatively young, who knows what the future holds? Sometimes even cemeteries go bankrupt!

Most cemeteries are nonprofit. When they're filling up,

it's their "working life," and when they're full, they're in retirement. States usually have a cash fund for perpetual care, keeping the place looking spiffy. But when a cemetery taps out and files for bankruptcy, it might end up deserted. Sometimes the community pitches in, but other times, graves might need a little relocation action.

Let's talk about coffin versus casket, because while the same concept, they're definitely not the same. A coffin is hexagon-shaped and meant to reflect the shape of a human body. It's tapered at the head and foot, wider at the shoulders. Before the mid-twentieth century, it was generally your only option. But now it's gone out of fashion for the most part, possibly because it's too morose for most. Although it's now considered old-school, it is still an option today.

A casket, on the other hand, is the smoother, more rectangular one you see in modern burials. They're usually built really beautifully and made of wood or metal, and some offer a mattress, pillow, blanket, and so on. However—you can go custom crazy and go out with a real bang. We're talking caskets shaped like motorcycles, race cars, airplanes, and so on. They can be decked out in your favorite hobby, sports team, or movie. Some have requested built-in sound systems to blast their favorite tunes on their way out. Possibilities! Are! Endless!

Here's one thing to consider when it comes to caskets: exploding caskets. It's a *thing*. When a body decomposes with a sealed casket, it releases gases as part of the natural decomposition process. Over time, the gases can build up within the sealed casket, and in rare cases—they fucking explode.

One more consideration: the runaway casket. Yes, sometimes caskets slide, slip, or take off down a hill! Madison has personal experience with this one: My beloved grandmother Frances passed away in hospice care on Christmas Day about twenty years ago. My family and I got an up-close and personal understanding of end-of-life care, but death was scary to me and a whole lot to process. We sat around her bed after she took her final breaths and watched as her wrinkles began to smooth out and a stillness took over. I, however, was not warned that a few days later I would be seeing her again wearing makeup and dressed in a fancy outfit in a big oak casket . . . which is when I was first introduced to the concept of a wake.

After the wake and funeral, it was off to the cemetery for burial. Her plot is in a cemetery that overlooks Los Angeles, surrounded by rolling green hills. Her casket was placed on a lowering mechanism at her grave. Catholic prayers started, and reality set in that this would be the last time I'd see my grandma . . . or so I thought (we will get to that in a later chapter). My grandma was funny as all get-out, and I think she decided to lighten the somber mood because suddenly her casket began sliding off the rails, heading for the bottom of the hill. One of my cousins leaped into action, stopping her casket from its downhill descent, and saved the day. I remember hearing gasps, and then the relief of laughter, and a few comments about how it looked like bobsledding. Thanks, Grandma!

Cremation: Ashes to ashes and dust to dust. During cremation, the body is subjected to heat so intense it turns every part of the body into an ashy dust. It's a fiery farewell and a space-saving option, to boot.

The current rate of cremation in the United States stood at 56 percent in 2020, so more than half. The Statista Research department estimates that the figure will be closer to 72.8 percent by 2030, which is pretty reasonable given that in 2010 the cremation rate was only at 40.59 percent. That's crazy how in just ten years there's been an almost 16 percent increase. Maybe they heard about the exploding caskets and said fuck that.

Donation: Instead of going through the hoopla of having to preserve your whole body, you can choose to donate your organs, tissues, or your whole body to science. It's the gift that keeps on giving, even after you're gone.

Natural burial: Skip the chemicals and fancy coffins and opt for a natural burial. Your body decomposes naturally, returning to the earth without leaving a big environmental footprint. There are biodegradable caskets and reforestation burials where remains can be used to fertilize and nurture young trees. The latest in natural burial innovation are mushroom suits, designed to promote decomposition and enrich the soil, supporting plant growth and creating a healthier ecosystem. This process doesn't require embalming, which involves the use of toxic chemicals.

Cryonics: This option offers a glimmer of hope for the eternal optimists among us. It's a process where your body is cooled down to a temperature so low that biological processes practically come to a standstill, with the expectation that future technology might revive you.

The process ideally begins with a proactive approach. If you're interested in cryopreservation and fortunate enough not to experience an unexpected demise, it's recommended to contact the facility you're a member of and inform them of your illness. They can be on standby to respond at the time of your death, ready to initiate the preserving process.

Upon legal declaration of your death, a crucial sequence of steps follows. Your cells and, ideally, most of your organs should still be viable. You'll be injected with an anticoagulant, often around thirty thousand units of Heparin, which is a prescription blood thinner. This prevents blood clots, an essential step for both living and deceased individuals.

Chest compressions commence for approximately five minutes or longer to ensure the even distribution of the anticoagulant throughout your body. Following this, immediate cooling begins, often involving an ice bath, with a particular focus on your head (containing your brain). In some cases, a body bag filled with ice is utilized for this purpose.

You'll then be transported to the cryonics facility of your choice, where in-house operating rooms come into play. The vitrification process is executed, starting with a thoracotomy procedure to open your chest. This provides access to your heart and allows the removal of all your blood and water from your cells. Cryoprotectant agents, essentially medical-grade antifreeze, replace your blood in a process called perfusion.

This step prevents ice or crystallization formation, which could damage your cells.

After the complete process, your body is cooled down to approximately -196 degrees Celsius (-321 degrees Fahrenheit) for about a week. You become frozen and solid, yet your insides remain preserved without crystallization, preventing decay and deterioration.

Finally, you are ready for your long-term resting place—a large tank filled with freezing liquid nitrogen. You'll remain there until society advances enough to potentially revive you. Currently, the means to revive cryonically preserved individuals haven't been discovered, but proponents believe that nanotechnology could hold the key. Nanoscopic repair devices might one day access cells, regenerate and repair tissues, and address the illnesses that contributed to the person's death.

In terms of cost, it's worth noting that cryonics comes at a price:

- A minimum of $80,000 for brain preservation.
- A minimum of $200,000 for whole-body preservation.
- Some family deals offer a 50 percent discount for multiple members.
- Cryonics for pets is only available to members, as they aim to reunite the animal with their family in the future.

Mummification: Channel your inner Egyptian pharaoh and undergo mummification. Your body is carefully preserved with drying agents and wraps, making you an artful relic for centuries to come. The number of mummifications in Egypt significantly decreased between the fourth and seventh century AD when many Egyptians converted to Christianity.

Body farm: For the scientifically curious, you can donate your body to a body farm, where forensic experts study decomposition in various conditions to help solve crimes. It's kind of what it sounds like: a legit farm with acres of land but instead of growing bodies they are decaying them. Body farms are research facilities that allow forensic anthropologists to witness and study a real-life human corpse decaying. These corpses are donated for scientific purposes, and thus, the bodies are all kind of doing something different for scientists to observe.

Allow us to set the scene:

You have a body laid out naked on their back in the middle of the field.

You have another body fully clothed and laid on their stomach.

You have some bodies lying on the ground inside of a cage, protecting them from vultures and other critters.

Some look like straight-up beef jerky and others are being fully eaten by maggots.

Others have even decayed fully and are just bones.

We're trying to imagine thinking, *I'm going to donate my body to science*, and then they ship you off to a farm and you're like naked in a field with maggots all over you. YIKES.

No, but in all seriousness, we know this all sounds really creepy and straight out of a horror film. The smell must be horrendous. But body farms are actually really very important. The first body farm was founded in East Tennessee in 1987 by an anthropologist named William Bass. Bass explained in an interview how on a body farm, anthropologists are able to study different effects on a human corpse like the elements surrounding them, weather, animals, plants, etc. They are also able to set up controlled scenes like what would happen to a body that was decaying inside of a trailer (there was a trailer set up on the farm, with, you guessed it, rotting corpses inside). Or what happens when a body is wrapped in a big black plastic garbage bag? Or what happens when a husband kills his wife and hides her under a bed or buries her in their backyard and pours concrete over it?

This is crucial information that seems morbid AF. However, it helps investigators in solving a lot of unsolved murders, aids in the handling of a crime scene and crime scene removal, and gives us a more accurate timeline when trying to discover when someone might have died.

The largest body farm in the United States is a forensic research facility in Texas. One anthropologist said that when a body is decaying on grass, the grass around it will die and create something called a death silhouette. Once the body has decayed, the grass will grow back even stronger and taller than the surrounding grass. She also talked about the way we have approached crime scenes in the past ten to twenty years by thinking, *Well, this crime happened outside, let's pick up everything and go.* And due to the removal, all the important context is lost. There is so much information just from the land where the body was discovered. For example, was the person killed in that location or brought to that location? Body farms give us the answers.

Memorial diamonds: Yep, you can have your ashes turned into a beautiful diamond that can be worn or kept as a family heirloom. Nowadays there's plenty of independent jewelers offering to memorialize your loved ones in a wearable piece, a ton on Etsy, as well as several larger companies that have thrown their hats in the ring. Perhaps one of the more well-known companies is LifeGem, who will turn your loved one into a diamond, and we just think it's so cool! They can do this with your pets as well! LifeGem offers a wide variety of diamonds, including blue, red, and colorless. As far as pricing goes, it depends on how large you want the gem and how many you want made; some people will do multiple diamonds for family members. According to LifeGem's website, from just eight ounces of cremated remains, they can extract enough carbon to make multiple diamonds. On average it takes about six to nine months to create a LifeGem diamond. If your loved one isn't cremated you can even use a lock of their hair in place of cremains—science, man!

Talk about a sparkly afterlife!

Tattoo preservation: Charles Hamm, a Tattooed Trailblazer and chairman of NAPSA (National Association for the Preservation of Skin Art), is who we have to thank for this one. Charles and his buddies were having a chat one day, and he's like, "Hey, guys, when I go, my tattoos are just gonna vanish in a puff of smoke!" Now, this bugged Charles to no end because he is no ordinary tattoo enthusiast. He's got some super sentimental ink dedicated to his better half and grand-kids, and he was on a mission to ensure these artistic stories lived on forever. That's where NAPSA comes in—it's all about keeping your tattoo tales alive for generations to come.

So, Charles joined forces with two tattoo wizards, Chuck Galati and Trevor Trentine, and brought a doctor and an embalmer into the mix. Charles was so dedicated to the cause that he even shed some extra weight so he'd have some loose skin that needed to go in the name of science.

He swung by a plastic surgeon's office, had that extra loose tattooed skin removed. Next stop, the embalmer! They took the freshly peeled inked skin, preserved it like a work of art, and voilà—an awesome experiment was born.

Charles proudly declares that it all worked like a charm, but here's the scoop: NAPSA's preservation magic is not on the menu for the living. Charles was the brave guinea pig who tried it out to make sure everything went smoothly.

Charles and his team weren't the only ones to go down this road. There are a handful of companies who specialize in turn-ing tattoos into forever works of art. It ain't cheap! A complete arm sleeve will run you between $5,000 and $7,500. A full chest or back goes for $15,000 to $20,000. In the end, loved ones of the deceased will end up with a UV-protected glass frame encasing the craziest works of art we've ever heard of.

So, whether you want to be embalmed, turned into ashes, ink, a freaking firework (true story), or even transformed into a dazzling gem, there are plenty of unique ways to decide what happens to your body in the end.

EXTREMELY EMBALMED

OHIO BIKER'S UNIQUE BURIAL WISH FULFILLED

In a truly extraordinary tribute to an Ohio biker's dying wish, Billy Standley was laid to rest perched upon his cherished 1967 Harley-Davidson, encased in a massive transparent casket. Mr. Standley, who had been battling lung cancer, spent years meticulously planning this distinctive burial with the help of his devoted sons, Pete and Roy.

Upon his passing, at the age of eighty-two, Mr. Standley's unconventional send-off was realized. Clad in his leather riding attire and iconic sunglasses, he was placed atop his beloved 1967 Electra Glide cruiser for one final ride to the beyond. What made this spectacle even more unique was the transparent plexiglass coffin, allowing mourners to view the rider's final journey.

Mr. Standley's preparations for his funeral were comprehensive. He purchased three adjoining burial plots beside his wife, Lorna, to ensure there was enough space for his unique casket. His sons, Pete and Roy, fashioned the transparent casket using plexiglass, reinforcing the bottom with wood and metal to ensure his stability. Additionally, to prevent any unsettling movement during his final journey, embalmers equipped Mr. Standley with a metal back brace and straps.

Tammy Vernon, a staff member at the funeral home, remarked, "We've done personalization . . . but nothing this extreme. He was the one who kept throwing this idea out there, to be buried on his bike. We were glad to assist him."

Mr. Standley took great pride in his funeral arrangements and would proudly exhibit the custom casket, which had been stored in a garage for five years, to visitors.

Though the procession to the cemetery, where Mr. Standley's body was displayed before burial, might have been startling to some, his family was determined to honor their father's final wish.

Dorothy, his daughter, described her father as "a quirky man." Mr. Standley, a former bareback rodeo rider, was escorted to the ceremony by a procession of fellow bikers. Many mourners at the graveside even donned motorcycle jackets as they watched the oversize casket being gently lowered into its sizable plot. This unique and heartfelt farewell served as a testament to the man who rode through life on his own terms.

2

THE BIG DAY

What does one wear to their last party . . . ever? Before we jump into what to wear, one thing the average person wouldn't think about is *how* to wear it. Getting a body dressed isn't all that easy. Typically the clothes have to be cut down the back to properly fit. Think about this, the body isn't able to stand upright, so whatever is being put on has to be rolled and tucked. In other words, if you're opting for a Hervé Léger bandage dress, getting it to fit could be cumbersome, and your last look isn't likely to win any "Who wore it best?" contests.

Choosing a burial outfit is extremely personal. It has to be something that speaks to who you were. How do you want to be remembered? An outfit can tell a lot about a person. Were you super expressive? Or were you subtle and classic?

Did you lean toward a specific era with your outfits? Did you serve our country and wear a uniform? There's also a cultural aspect to it. Many cultures' burial outfits hold significant value and meaning.

For example, a Buddhist would typically be buried in something casual, nothing fancy or expensive, as they believe that you don't need to have elaborate, costly ceremonies for the end of life, it's just another part of the cycle.

For Muslims, according to our research, bodies are to be washed three times until entirely clean. Women's hair should be washed and braided into three braids. Once the body has gone through this ritual, the body will be covered in a white sheet. Women will be fitted in a sleeveless dress and head veil.

For the Jewish community, the deceased undergo a ritual process known as taharah. This refers to the cleansing of the body before burial. Prayers are read, strict protocols are adhered to, and a person of the same gender as the deceased handles their body. They are then dressed in cotton shrouds, unless they want to be buried in their regular clothing. Many men and some women also wear a prayer shawl.

Catholics typically go a little more formal in attire, as it could be seen as being disrespectful to underdress for Jesus. For the most part, in many Western and Christian cultures, traditional funeral attire includes dark and conservative clothing, such as suits or dresses. Black has been the most common color for many years, although in recent times, there's been a shift toward celebrating life rather than wallowing in death. In terms of style, this mindset encourages people to dress in lighter colors or clothing that reflects their—or their loved ones'—tastes and personality.

Speaking of personality, nobody has dressed for funerals quite like some of our favorite stars.

Aretha Franklin had probably the most fabulous funeral outfits—yes, we said outfits, plural. First of all, she had a gold-plated casket. And because she was such a huge star to so many, she had three public viewings before her private service!

For the first viewing, Aretha wore a red lace dress with red Louboutin heels, to match her red lips and nails. This was a nod to Delta Sigma Theta Sorority, of which she was an honorary member. At the second viewing, she wore all powder blue and matching blue heels. For the third viewing, she wore a rose-gold suit, with another pair of Louboutin shoes.

She was finally laid to rest in a long gold gown with matching heels. RESPECT.

Marilyn Monroe was buried in an avocado-green Emilio Pucci dress when she passed away in 1962. The elegant sheath had a long, narrow silhouette with a boatneck and three-quarter sleeves. It hit right at the knee. It has been said that her ex-husband, business partner, and close friend Joe DiMaggio selected the dress.

Elvis Presley was laid to rest in all white in 1977. For his public viewing, he wore a white jumpsuit, scarf, and gold belt. For his private funeral, it has been said he wore a white suit and tie, which was a departure from his flashy and elaborate stage costumes. True to his personal style, he reportedly wore his famous TCB ring and a bracelet.

Anna Nicole Smith's funeral is Madison's final party inspiration. As a nod to the model and actress's favorite color, it was all pink everything. Even the mourners were asked to wear pink. She was reportedly buried in a pink gown and tiara. Her casket was covered in rhinestones that spelled out her name. Love this look for Anna.

George H. W. Bush was buried in a classic suit, but it's been said he had special socks on. Apparently in his life, that was something he loved; different socks for every occasion! How cool is that? His burial socks had planes all over them to pay tribute to his time as a naval aviator and his time of service to the country.

GG Allin, an American punk rock singer and songwriter known for his controversial and extreme stage antics, passed away in 1993 from a heroin overdose. He was buried in a jockstrap and a leather jacket. He'd previously expressed a desire to be buried in his favorite outfit, and those wishes were honored. Props to GG's friends for carrying this wish through for him!

Zsa Zsa Gabor was actually cremated after she died in 2016. Her Beverly Hills funeral was small and intimate. While she didn't have a final resting outfit, her urn sure did. Her remains and the urn were kept in a gold box, which was placed in a Louis Vuitton dog carrier. When her husband gave his eulogy at the funeral, he explained that this carrier went everywhere with them, and he chose this to hold her urn because "dogs were her best people." He also explained that he took the urn with him for the speech because she would have said, "If you go onstage, I go onstage!"

Many people opt to be buried in their wedding dress. It's actually not that uncommon. This is probably because people want to be laid to rest in attire that holds sentimental value, and for some, their wedding dress represents a—if not the—most significant and cherished part of their life.

MOURNING WAREHOUSES

While the options for attire are endless today, it wasn't always that way. Bringing it back to the Victorian era, well, let's just say nobody was going out in a jockstrap. Mourning was meant to be dark and depressing, and those experiencing it were expected to stay in that space for a very long time. None of this *celebration of life* stuff we've embraced in later years. In fact, the mourning process was so hard-core, they had mourning warehouses, basically a Target for the death industry. These mega stores were popping up everywhere in the nineteenth centuries. Get in, losers, we're going shopping. . . .

Need stationery to express your condolences, funeral attire, or even a coffin? Check, check, check. Funeral invitations or rolls of black crepe? They had you covered. These one-stop funerary shops had it all! One of our favorite things one would have found at a mourning warehouse includes tear catchers. Also known as lachrymatories, or tear vials, these were small containers that were believed to collect the tears shed by mourners during times of grief. These delicate glass or ceramic vessels were usually ornately designed and came in various shapes and sizes. It became a tangible expression of grief one could hold on to, to demonstrate the depth of their emotions, as it was believed that capturing tears symbolized the depth of one's sorrow and love for the departed. Some even thought that evaporating tears were a way to send messages to the afterlife. We think these catchers are especially sweet because once the tears dried up, some would say it symbolized the end of mourning.

Funeral attire didn't just stop at the ceremony. Oh, no, those in mourning were in head-to-toe black for months. And because we're talking Victorian era, the everyday getup included gloves, veils, scarves, and so on.

Peter Robinson's Family Mourning Warehouse, part of the renowned Peter Robinson chain of department stores founded in 1833, gained popularity as a prominent establishment. In 1840, Peter Robinson extended the chain by establishing a dedicated mourning warehouse named Court and General Mourning House. To distinguish between the regular department stores and the mourning warehouse, the latter became known as Black Peter Robinson's.

Interestingly, historical records indicate that the mourning warehouse employed unique customer service practices. Notably, there was a horse-drawn carriage stationed outside the shop, complete with a coachman and an attendant ready to assist individuals seeking mourning attire at any time. These attendants were appropriately dressed in black, ready to respond promptly to calls from widows in need of mourning gear. As the business evolved, the mourning warehouse embraced modern technology. In 1892, a telephone was installed in the shop, enhancing their ability to conduct business efficiently.

Such innovative strategies were among the selling tactics employed by mourning warehouses during that era. An intriguing aspect of Peter Robinson's business legacy is the role it played in the creation of the iconic brand Topshop. Yes, the same store you can currently purchase pink patent leather platforms. Originally introduced as "Peter Robinson's Topshop" in 1964, the brand extension aimed to appeal to a younger and trendier demographic. However, by the 1970s, Peter Robinson and Topshop underwent a separation, leading to the discontinuation of the Peter Robinson brand while Topshop has continued to thrive as an independent entity for years and years and years to come.

Jay's Mourning Warehouse, established in 1841 by William Chickhall Jay, emerged as perhaps the largest and most renowned among mourning warehouses. Officially known as "the London General Mourning Warehouse," it became widely recognized as Jay's due to its popularity. Situated alongside Black Peter Robinson's on Regent Street in London, Jay's capitalized on the flourishing business of mourning, employing various selling tactics as several branches sprang up.

An interesting facet of Jay's Mourning Warehouse was its proactive approach to educating Victorian mourners. The establishment commissioned writer Richard Davey to author *A History of Mourning*, a comprehensive guidebook exploring mourning rituals from ancient times through the nineteenth century. This book served as a valuable resource for Jay's to enlighten their clientele on proper mourning protocols, covering everything from clothing and jewelry to coffins.

For the convenience of patrons unable to visit the store, Jay's implemented a catalog system. These catalogs featured fashionable outfits and decor for mourning, allowing customers to make selections remotely. Moreover, akin to Black Peter Robinson's, Jay's dispatched lady fitters to size customers for their mourning needs.

Jay's Mourning Warehouse prided itself on offering a comprehensive range of services. Customers could be fitted for mourning outfits at every stage of mourning, and the establishment provided funeral flowers. Notably, even Queen

Victoria, renowned as the queen of mourning, was counted among Jay's loyal clientele.

Speaking of Queen V, she was really the one who started this whole industry. Her own behavior, particularly after the death of her beloved husband, Prince Albert, set a precedent for others and had a profound influence on mourning rituals during the Victorian era. Her mourning period lasted for an exceptionally long time, like forty years long, and this influenced societal expectations, encouraging individuals to observe prolonged periods of mourning for their loved ones. Part of this period included Queen Victoria's preference for wearing black during her mourning period. This popularized the use of black clothing as a symbol of grief. This practice became a cultural norm, and individuals were expected to dress in black or other dark colors during mourning periods. The black attire worn by mourners became a visual representation of their sorrow.

The queen also displayed her mourning jewelry, particularly pieces containing locks of hair from the deceased. From this, mourning hair wreaths became popular. People would utilize the hair not only of the deceased but also their living loved ones. It was a display of an emotional connection to one another. You might see pictures from this era where the person has multiple colors of hair, and this is why—it was donated by different people, whether dead or alive. Mourning jewelry, often featuring somber symbols and materials like jet or onyx, also became a common way for individuals to express their grief and remember their loved ones.

Queen Victoria's elaborate funeral arrangements for

Prince Albert influenced the way funerals were conducted as well. This included the use of black-draped hearses, grand processions, strict burial instructions, and extensive mourning rituals. These practices were emulated by the upper and middle classes, shaping the expectations surrounding funeral ceremonies. She was serious when it came to etiquette, protocol, and the set standards for society. This included expectations for subdued behavior while mourning, such as refraining from social events and wearing specific mourning attire. The queen's commitment to these customs reinforced their importance in Victorian society.

Due to Queen Victoria's influence on the industry, she created a demand for mourning-related products and services. This led to the growth of a mourning industry, including mourning warehouses like Jay's and Black Peter Robinson's. Hope she got a good discount!

Suffice to say, Queen Victoria's approach to mourning became a model for societal behavior, shaping the mourning rituals and customs of the Victorian era and contributing to the development of a distinctive mourning culture during the nineteenth century, one that still continues in some (but not all) ways today.

One practice that has fortunately ended involves the use of crepe as a mourning ritual. You've probably noticed how ladies in movies have worn a black net fabric over their face, either from a hat or other headpiece (shout out to *Death Becomes Her*!). This style is a nod to a longtime custom for expressing grief and showing respect for the departed. The use of crepe is a fascinating yet discomforting aspect of Victorian mourning practices. Today, this crimped, crunchy material might not make much of a difference in our lives. It's used on tutus, modern dresses, and other frilly attire. But back in the day, this material could literally kill you.

Despite its significance in mourning attire, crepe had numerous downsides. It was expensive, uncomfortable, and stiff. On top of that, the fabric emitted an unpleasant odor and had a tendency to bleed dye, especially in rainy or humid conditions. The pure, deep-black dye that crepe could achieve made it an ideal choice for heavy mourning, but this came at the cost of many inconveniences. Can you imagine you leave the house looking fine and, upon returning, your face is covered in black ink?

Crepe went beyond clothing and found its way into mourning symbolism. It was hung on doorknobs and draped at entrances to signify mourning within households. Women even carried crepe fans, contributing to the visual language of grief. The common phrase "There is crepe on the door" was used in obituaries and stories of tragic deaths and became a common expression of mourning.

The use of crepe in mourning attire had serious health implications. To remove stains left by the fabric on the skin, a mixture of oxalic acid and cream of tartar was applied—an unhealthy practice by today's standards. Moreover, the crepe fabric itself contained toxic elements like copper chloride, chromium, and arsenic. Long-term exposure to these substances through the shedding of dust particles from crepe veils could lead to skin conditions, respiratory problems, vision disorders, and, in extreme cases, even death. DEATH!

It was considered bad luck to keep mourning veils and clothing in the home once the traditional full mourning period was over. As a result, women had to purchase new mourning attire for each family member's passing, contributing to the economic aspects of the mourning industry. Enter the booming success of mourning warehouses.

And, sad as it is to say, people in the Victorian era spent a lot of time mourning. When it came to the children of the nineteenth century, things like cholera, scarlet fever, smallpox, and typhoid were just a number of afflictions that ended one's life early on. Many of these diseases left people in pretty bad shape, and embalming wasn't like it is today. To mourn children, grave dolls came into the picture. These were life-size, usually wax effigies of children, many times wearing the deceased children's clothes. The dolls were made with flat backs so they could sit in a coffin or even a frame. They were displayed at the gravesite of a child and also in the home as a memorial. Many times, these dolls were kept in cribs in the family's home. One of you is thinking about turning this into a scary movie screenplay right now—please name a character after us. Thanks.

Today, in America, that is, we may have (sometimes) kept the color black, but otherwise, tend to keep things simple across the board, and with plenty of room for creativity. You can be buried in whatever you wish. You don't have to dress how you feel. You can mourn how you see fit. Your mourning period ends when you say it ends. While we respect the history of mourning, we welcome this later mentality with open arms.

FUNERAL MEALS

Before we bounce on this topic, we'd like to address one of the most important aspects to any gathering, in our opinion: What's for lunch?

Food actually has a major role in relation to loss. When Spencer's mom passed away a few years ago, he was surrounded by the absolute best people who were so kind and really just infiltrated his family with thoughtfulness during a really hard time. Spencer actually made a list in the Notes app on his phone because he wanted to remember what people did for him, and we've referenced that list several times when other people we know have lost a loved one. This includes comforting things people have said to acts of service. Should you ever find yourself in a position where you want to help but don't know how, we got you!

In the first week following her passing, friends dropped off breakfast pretty much every day—pastries, bagels, orange juice, coffee. The same occurred for dinner. Sending someone a meal is one of the simplest but most important things you can do because the last thing anyone grieving is thinking about is what to do for dinner. You're in a place where you don't want to leave the house, and to have sustenance show up is incredibly helpful.

So meals, coffees, and snacks are super helpful. Another

thing a few people did was send us gift cards for food-delivery services. It's such a nice way to say, *Hey, I care about you. Take care of yourself by ordering something good for dinner.*

And that leads us to yukgaejang, which is a traditional Korean dish. It's a spicy beef soup with scallions, bean sprouts, garlic, sweet potatoes, and chili, and is usually served with a bowl of rice and kimchi. During Korean funeral services, family members actually use the soup as part of a ritual where the deceased person is offered bowls of rice and then they place three spoonfuls of the yukgaejang into the deceased's mouth.

Many Jewish people will have something called Seudat Havara'ah, a.k.a. the first meal. This is consumed by the mourning family on their return from the burial. It is considered a private meal to be shared among immediate family members, not a public event where condolences are offered. The Seudat Havara'ah or "meal of comfort" is provided by friends, family, or members of the community, and typically consists of peeled hard-boiled eggs and some variation of the lentil stew that, according to the Talmud, Jacob was preparing for his father, Isaac, who was mourning for his own father, Abraham. These foods—especially the round hard-boiled eggs—symbolize the cycle of life and are traditionally followed by the delivery of condolence baskets and local deli platters for the duration of the weeklong shiva period.

During Día de los Muertos, a.k.a. Day of the Dead, Mexican families have traditionally eaten pan de muerto, which are these sweet bread rolls, many of them have a cross on top and are generally topped with sugar or decorated with some kind of sweet treat. Families will visit their loved ones' final resting place and share them as an oferenda (Spanish for "offering") to the spirit of their loved ones. Many also put these sweets on the ofrenda (a ceremonial altar) at their home with the pictures of deceased loved ones along with orange and yellow marigolds, which represent the sun and symbolize life.

At an Irish wake you'll find what's called an Irish wake cake, which is traditionally made with butter, eggs, cream cheese, cake flour, vanilla extract, baking powder, salt, and buttermilk—pretty much everything you'd find in a traditional cake recipe but also with some unexpected ingredients like dried currants or raisins and lemon juice.

Traditional funeral meals in America also depend on the region that you're in. Across the board, most have charcuterie boards to snack on and appetizers like stuffed mushrooms and veggie or fruit trays. In the Midwest, it's common to serve egg salad sandwiches, and you best believe they'll have a hot dish waiting for you. Now, in the South, you'll get a spread, honey. From baked macaroni and cheese to ham biscuits, fried chicken, collard greens, to a plethora of different casseroles. Personally, we are huge advocates of eating your feelings.

We can't talk about all this food without offering up a recipe, right? Here's one of our favorites:

Funeral potatoes, also known as "Mormon funeral potatoes," are a popular and comforting casserole dish that is often served at gatherings, potlucks, and, as the name suggests, funeral receptions in some regions, particularly among the

Latter-day Saint (LDS) community. The dish has become a staple in the western United States and is known for its rich and hearty flavors.

The base of the dish is usually shredded or diced potatoes. Hash browns are commonly used for convenience—and we are here for that. A creamy and flavorful sauce binds the dish together. The sauce typically consists of ingredients like sour cream, cream-of-mushroom soup, or cream-of-chicken soup. Funeral potatoes are often loaded with cheese for extra richness. Cheddar cheese is a popular choice, but variations may use other types of cheese as well. As far as toppings go, to each their own. We've found variations like cornflakes, crushed crackers, or bread crumbs to add a crunchy texture to the top layer when baked.

Here's a basic recipe for funeral potatoes, a comforting and hearty casserole. Keep in mind we aren't in the Victorian days of lore and you can customize this recipe to suit your tastes.

FUNERAL POTATOES

1 package (about 30 ounces) frozen shredded hash browns, thawed

½ cup unsalted butter, melted

1 can (10.5 ounces) cream-of-chicken soup

2 cups sour cream

1 small onion, finely chopped

2 cups shredded sharp cheddar cheese

Salt and pepper to taste

2 cups cornflakes, crushed (for topping)

INSTRUCTIONS

1. Preheat your oven to 350°F (175°C). Grease a 9 x 13-inch baking dish.
2. Prepare the potatoes. If you haven't already, thaw the frozen hash browns and spread them evenly in the prepared baking dish.
3. In a large mixing bowl, combine the melted butter, cream-of-chicken soup, sour cream, chopped onion, and shredded cheddar cheese. Season with salt and pepper to taste. Mix until well combined.
4. Pour the sauce mixture over the thawed hash browns in the baking dish. Gently fold the mixture until the hash browns are evenly coated.
5. Crush the cornflakes and sprinkle them evenly over the top of the casserole. The crushed cornflakes add a nice crunch to the dish.
6. Place the baking dish in the preheated oven and bake for approximately 45–50 minutes, or until the top is golden brown, and the casserole is hot and bubbly.
7. Allow the funeral potatoes to cool for a few minutes before serving. This dish is often served as a side dish and pairs well with various main courses.

3

FUNerals

Honestly, funerals used to be kinda lit, especially in China, where they included musical performances and dancing. It was much more of a to-do. In Greece, they used to hold funeral games to honor and commemorate the deceased. This allegedly evolved into what we now know as the Olympics. It seems a lot of cultures put the fun in funerals, as it is way more of a celebration than a sad card table with a single vase on it. . . . But then, again there is no wrong way to mourn, *your funeral is your funeral* vibe. For example, Elizabeth Taylor requested that she be fashionably late to her own funeral. Love her for this. In our opinion, the most stressful thing about hosting any event boils down to one question: What if nobody shows up?

Enter one of the strangest jobs out there: moirologists

(moy-raw-lo-gists). Perhaps better known as wailers or professional mourners, these are individuals or groups who are essentially paid to come to a funeral and assist the friends and family of a deceased loved one in mourning their death. You can literally pay someone to cry and threaten to jump into the grave, if you are so inclined. They charge more for this, of course.

In some places, professional mourners would tear their clothes, pull out their hair, all while screaming and crying, very theatrical. This started as a practice for the wealthy, who thought it made the deceased's family look more regal or prominent, especially in regards to the extreme theatrical performances. Imagine looking down at your own funeral and seeing all of these randoms in attendance—sobbing.

The origin of the practice of employing professional mourners can be traced back to China, where some form of this tradition has been in use since the year 756 and continues to be utilized today. This custom has also been historically present in Egypt and throughout the majority of the Middle East.

In ancient times, the role of a moirologist was mostly limited to women, due to societal expectations that men, as strong leaders, should not openly express emotion. This perception persisted until the 1970s, when societal views began to shift, although remnants of such stereotypes linger.

Over time, the role of moirologists evolved, becoming more subdued. They started attending funerals to quietly cry, while some were compensated for delivering eulogies or paying respects to the departed. The popularity and prevalence of professional mourners have varied across different cultures and time periods. While the practice may have been more common in certain historical periods, it is important to note that it has not always been universally practiced or accepted.

The tradition of hiring mourners has persisted in some cultures, but its popularity has fluctuated over time. In contemporary societies, the practice of employing professional mourners may still be observed in certain regions or communities, albeit not as widespread as in ancient times.

In the Victorian era in England, the practice took a more quantifiable turn, with the number of attendees at a funeral seen as an indicator of the deceased's importance, which makes sense, since the hiring of moirologists had always happened for various reasons. This could be driven by concerns about low attendance, a desire to enhance the perceived importance or popularity of the deceased, or to prevent the sadness of a sparsely attended funeral. They're basically method actors, emphasizing the need to authentically play the part, as families often prefer to keep the hiring of actors for such purposes discreet. And can we just say, somebody hand these guys an Oscar because—wow. That's a lot of emotion and a tough job.

Anyway, if you feel so inclined to hire professional mourners for your funeral, expect to pay a hefty price. The cost usually ranges between $35 an hour all the way up to $500, which we are assuming for the latter you get the person threatening to jump into the grave.

But even beyond the professional actors, there always seems to be some drama surrounding a funeral . . . pending wills, lookie-loos, ex-wives, suspicious circumstances, and so on. But let us tell you, babe, that ain't nothing. The dearly deceased is already dealing with much bigger issues like death erections and exploding caskets (see chapter 1). And let us not forget grave robbing or necrophilia—rest in peace no more. It's no wonder some people opt to make their funeral . . . fun. The most extreme scenarios: such as Judy Sunday, a woman whose casket mourners threw down a bowling lane; New Orleans socialite Mickey Easterling, who was arranged posing with a glass of champs in one hand and a cigarette in the other; or Miriam Burbank, who was positioned at a table with beer, whiskey, and cigarettes. Why have a funeral when you can have a FUNeral, babe?

While funerals are generally solemn occasions meant for mourning and remembrance, some individuals and families cannot imagine going out that way because it's just not . . . them. We get it. Nobody wants to throw a boring party. Many have hired DJs, magicians, and even dancing pallbearers to provide an element of entertainment. A rare but real thing are funeral clowns—yes, clowns—meant to provide entertainment and lighten the mood in order to help mourners cope with their grief.

But nothing prepared us for funeral strippers! Also a very real thing. Funeral strippers are just that, exotic dancers who sing and dance while removing their clothes at a funeral or in a procession to a funeral as a way to celebrate the life of the deceased and attract mourners. See! Everyone is afraid nobody will show up to their last party! If strippers can't bring 'em in—what will, really? The tradition originated in Taiwan

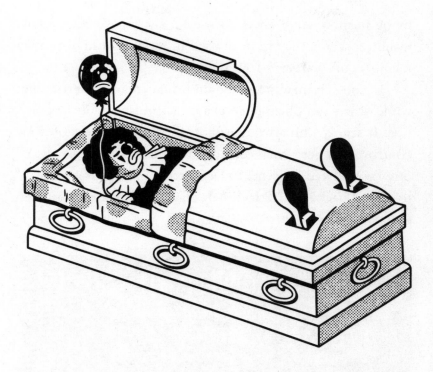

and has since spread throughout parts of China. Some say it brings good luck. We're not experts here, but we're willing to bet those people are straight men. Something that makes sense: the practice began in the 1980s when gangsters assumed control of the mortuary industry and offered strippers from their clubs to mourners at a respectfully discounted price.

In Chinese culture, they take funerals very seriously, which is easy to understand since their culture is all for respecting their elders and ancestors. Traditionally they make funerals a big deal. Based on our research, it seems funeral strippers are more often hired by the working class, people living in more rural areas. However, there have been a few instances where they've been used in services of high-profile members of society, so who knows.

As you can imagine, some find the dancing entertaining while others can't help but feel a little uneasy about the practice. It seems China has significantly cracked down on this controversial performance, since this little strip tease act is often considered obscene. In fact, they started giving rewards to people back in 2018 to snitch on others for hiring funeral strippers.

GOING OUT IN STYLE

Mary Cathryn "Mickey" Easterling, noted philanthropist, Patron of the Arts, and one of the last New Orleans "Grande Dames" of her generation, went peacefully to her eternal rest at home on April 14, 2014, after a lengthy illness. Her age? Mickey always said, "Age is a number, and mine's unlisted." She is survived by her son, Ed Easterling, of Corvallis, Oregon, and daughter, Nanci Easterling, of New Orleans.

We're not sure there's ever been a more iconic entry to an obituary, she is unlisted, babe!

The obituary went on to detail our gal Mickey's love for the arts and her worldly travels, giving a nod to her hospitable nature, writing: *She was noted for the wonderful and very well attended parties and dinners she hosted for friends and acquaintances from around the world.*

Summarizing Mickey's gracious nature, they ended the obituary with:

She helped a lot of people, especially children suffering from illness, and local artists and musicians trying to make a breakthrough with their talent. She was a gracious hostess to everyone from the rich and famous, to the little-known artists and musicians of the French Quarter who were struggling to merely survive. She was a wonderful friend to people the world over, and a major contributor to New Orleans's charitable, arts, music, and cultural activities and facilities. She will be missed.

Darling, don't be afraid to be original. —Mickey Easterling

PART 2

YOU CAN'T HANDLE
THE TRUTH

4

WHAT REMAINS

Picture this: You hit your expiration date, shuffle off this mortal coil, and head to the great beyond. But before you go, you want to make sure your stuff ends up in the right hands. So you whip out your trusty last will and testament, where you can spill the beans on who gets what, how you wanna be laid to rest (or maybe do something wild instead), and what to do with your beloved sweater collection. It's like a final power move from beyond the grave!

Now, most last wills are pretty ho-hum affairs, but oh boy, throughout history, we've had some real characters who took it to the next level. Cue the drumroll for none other than the master escape artist himself, Harry Houdini! This guy was no ordinary magician, mind you. When he shuffled off to the other side, he left behind a will that had a twist of eccentricity. You see, he had this strange clause in there for his wife, Bess Houdini.

Harry insisted that every year, without fail, Bess should hold a séance to try to reach out to him from the great beyond. But wait, it gets even better! While he was still breathing and performing his jaw-dropping acts, Harry had given Bess a secret list of random words. The idea was that if someone managed to connect with the spirit realm, they would utter those secret words, and boom! It would be like Harry himself was whispering from the other side.

So Bess, being the trooper she was, kept up this spine-tingling tradition for a solid ten years by inviting the world's most renowned psychics, mediums, and spiritual experts to an annual séance. Can you imagine? A yearly gathering of eager attendees, hanging on to every whisper in the hope of hitting the spiritual jackpot and channeling Houdini's magic mojo. But alas, after a decade of fervent attempts, she eventually threw in the towel and called it quits.

And then we have the legendary Charles Vance Millar, a true master of the unexpected. In the roaring 1920s, this man left behind a will that could rival the wildest reality TV show. Brace yourselves for the "Great Stork Derby"! Charles bequeathed a sizable chunk of his estate to the Toronto woman who popped out the most children within a specific period. That's right, folks, he turned procreation into a full-blown competition! Can you imagine the chaos that ensued as women vied for the ultimate prize? It was like a baby-making marathon with a fortune on the finish line. Talk about raising the stakes!

But Charles isn't the only one who knew how to make a splash from beyond the grave. Back in 1832, we had the delightfully morbid Jeremy Bentham, an English philosopher and social reformer who took eccentricity to a whole new level. This guy knew how to leave a lasting impression—literally! In his last will, he made a rather peculiar request: he wanted his body to be preserved, seated in a chair, wearing his snazzy clothes. Rumors are that he even carried glass eyeballs in his pocket so his embalmer would be ready to pop them in his noggin! The preservation of his body went swimmingly but his head looked like a football with glass eyes. Instead of using his real head, he was fortunately topped off with a wax replica that looked just like him pre-preservation.

This strange arrangement, my friends, was aptly called an "auto-icon." And guess what? You can catch a glimpse of Jeremy's preserved self at University College London. Yup, he's there for all to see, a true testament to the extraordinary wonders of the human imagination. Speaking of human imagination, his real head was allegedly stolen a few times by students and used as an actual football.

That's just a taste of the wild and wacky world of last wills and testaments. From baby bonanzas to wax-headed philosophers, these eccentric departures from the norm remind us that life—and even death—can be a wild and unpredictable adventure. And we haven't even started talking about pets. Imagine being the direct descendant of a bazillionaire and only after they're gone you find out the entire fortune has been left to the dogs. Literally.

Hotel magnate Leona Helmsley famously left very clear instructions in her will that after her passing, in 2007, the majority of her trust should be left to her beloved pets. In the trust's mission statement, Leona specified the trust was to be used only for the care and welfare of her pups. Guaranteed those dogs ate better than us. Her human grandchildren were excluded from the will, and the other family members shared a combined inheritance of $10 million. But her nine-year-old Maltese, Trouble, received $12 million. If that wasn't enough, it was allegedly in Leona's will that when Trouble died, she would lie beside her owner in the twelve-thousand-square-foot Helmsley family mausoleum in Sleepy Hollow Cemetery in Westchester County, New York. That mausoleum was to be "washed or steam-cleaned at least once a year," for which she left $3 million.

For the most part, people see their last will as their final words of *I love you* or a big fat *screw you*. They're completely generous, making sure things are even for siblings or children, and making sure everyone feels cared for and seen. That, or they're sticking it to someone by excluding them completely, or making their trust more of a challenge, like the Londoner who willed his fortune to his sons on the strict condition they wouldn't inherit anything if they became members of Parliament or any public office, partake in the stock exchange, convert to another religion, or marry outside the Jewish faith. Helicopter parent much? Or poet Heinrich Heine, who vowed to give everything to his widowed wife on the condition that she remarried. This might sound sweet but in truth, he was being kind of a dick. His wife was known to be boring and vain. Heine actually said that if she remarried, "there will be at least one man who will regret my death." Burn.

We like wealthy people like Luis Carlos de Noronha Cabral de Camara, who wrote in his will he wasn't sure who to include in his list of beneficiaries. He didn't have children and only had a few friends, so he took an awesome approach—in our opinion. He chose seventy names at random from the phone book! These surprised heirs took home around seven thousand euros each. Pretty cool.

Last wills are kind of like your last hurrah, your last little secret to reveal. It's a final opportunity to make them think,

I wonder if Aunt Jane left me that painting I've always wanted. Surprise! She did. *I wonder if Grandma is giving me anything from what's left of her estate. What the fuck—she left it to the cat?!*

At one point Madison thought she would never see her deceased Grandma again. My runaway-casket grandma (see page 13) was married to my sweet grandpa for fifty-plus years. He passed very shortly after her, leaving behind so many special, meaningful heirlooms that my mom and her sister had to divvy up. I didn't receive any of those, instead I inherited his 2001 Dell PC. I was just excited to have a computer, and I started exploring what this huge thing had to offer! Soon, I was teary-eyed, looking through photos of their cherished life together until I stumbled upon photos of my grandma in her casket! UM, WHAT?! Despite the initial shock, I understood my grandpa's deep love for my grandma, seeking to hold on to her memory even in death.

SENICIDE

While we're on the topic of grandparents it seems like the perfect time to discuss senicide. By definition, senicide is the killing of the elderly or their abandonment to death. Essentially senicide has been practiced by several different cultures throughout history, with some believing that it's a form of assisted death.

We'll start with the practice of Thalaikoothal, which hails from the southern Indian state of Tamil Nadu, where the practice is alleged to occur dozens of times per year, though some sources claim it's more like hundreds! And we know killing = bad, but in an attempt at thinking with an open mind, we think (or hope) communities practicing senicide are looking at it through the lens of something like death with dignity, usually when people are too old to be able to care for themselves. According to one article from *The Week*, based in India, "In Thalaikoothal, the body is massaged with 100ml each of coconut, castor and sesame oils, usually at dawn. After this, the person is given a cold bath and put to bed. The body temperature soon dips, often to a lethal extent. After 15 minutes, the person is made to drink a few glasses of tender coconut water and a glass of milk. This causes renal failure. In a day or two, the person catches a fever and dies. All the way up until a few years ago, if the oil and coconut water cocktail failed to do the trick, the person would be given a glass of mud mixed with water or a piece of murukku, a savory [snack], would be forced down the throat essentially causing them to choke to death."

Though villagers claim they have buried this gruesome tradition, it has now taken on a silent form. Unlike earlier, when it was socially acceptable, relatives are no longer informed or invited. As if that's not bad enough, we need to discuss the evolution of the ritual. Nowadays pesticides, sleeping pills, and lethal injections have become go-to methods in the dated practice. Some local doctors even prescribe Valium tablets. Japan has its own custom known as ubasute where elderly relatives would be carried to a mountain or somewhere just absolutely in the middle of nowhere and left there to die. LIKE WHAT? There was even a novel about it written in 1956 by Shichiro Fukazawa called *The Ballad of Narayama*.

Further research has shown that senicide was common among the Inuit in northern Alaska and Greenland. Based on what we've researched, senicide was rare except during famines. As long as there was enough food to go around, everyone got their share, including the relatively unproductive. Given that the usual diet consisted of fairly dependable catches of caribou, fish, and sea mammals, many years could pass between episodes of scarcity. Far more commonly they were simply abandoned to die. The victim might be taken out in the wilderness and left there, or the whole village might pick up and move away while the old person slept. If the villagers were unexpectedly restored to prosperity, they might go back to rescue those left behind. An abandoned person would also be welcomed back as a full member of the community if he could manage to make his way back to the village on his own. But usually he couldn't.

In Sardinia's past they would allegedly throw their sick elders off certain cliffs. Sometimes senicide would be done by a select group of women named accabadoras, a.k.a. the terminators or enders. They would bless them and then proceed to either suffocate them, or kill them with blunt-force trauma by hitting them on the back of the head with a wooden mallet.

A lot of these practices are real old, and some have merely become folklore, but the idea of just dropping off Grandpa at the mountain and being like, *Alrighty kids, wave goodbye!!!!* is absolutely wild to us!

ONCE UPON A CRIME

This funeral home scandal is twisted, conniving, and has all the makings of a Hollywood movie.

In 1929, a man named Charles Lamb built a large funeral home in Pasadena, California. We've seen photos of the beautiful Spanish mission-style building on the corner of Orange Grove Boulevard. Inside was a stunning parlor filled with sofas and armchairs to allow grieving families to sit in comfort as they discussed their plans for the deceased with Charles. It was big news at the time, and the new funeral home was welcomed by the city of Pasadena. In November 1929, it was front-page news: "CF Lamb Funeral Home to open for inspection tomorrow"; a big headline: "Beautiful new mortuary captures charm."

Charles was a big deal; he'd worked in the industry for more than twenty years and held a position as president of the state's Funeral Directors Association. He and his wife catered to the Pasadena community for several decades before eventually passing off the family business to their son, Lawrence. Lawrence continued on in his father's footsteps and ensured that the family business maintained its level of professionalism and care as it had since the first day of operation. Eventually he ended up working as president of the Pasadena school board and passed the business off to one of his daughters, Laurieanne. Well, technically she bought it; she pooled together $65,000 as a down payment to buy her father out. A quote on Laurieanne from the *Los Angeles Times*:

"Laurieanne, one of Lawrence's two daughters, was bright and so pretty that a rival mortician would describe her as 'movie star beautiful.'" She carried herself with a touch of gentility befitting the family's position in the community, sprinkled her conversations liberally with biblical quotations, and wrote sacred songs for her own gospel group, the Chapebelles. Her father's favorite, she demonstrated a gift for consoling survivors at the mortuary, some of whom gave her money to save for their own funerals!

We picture Laurieanne as like Cousin Marilyn from *The Munsters*, like the pretty gal around ghouls. She loved working at the funeral home and even did the makeup on some of the deceased visitors.

Prior to taking over the family business, she had been attending college and dropped out to marry Jerry Sconce, a football player at UC Santa Barbara, and apparently he was kind of a loser, being that he was a cheater and a gambler. But on paper he was great. He ran a sporting goods store around the time Laurieanne took over the funeral home, and just before her twentieth birthday they had welcomed a son, David. This is where our story really begins. David Sconce was a lot like his dad. After graduating from high school in Glendora, he enrolled at the Christian college where his father was working as a coach at the time. During his freshman year, his girlfriend broke up with him, and in turn he robbed her house, not once but twice. That's just the tip of the iceberg. He was a real dirtbag who would go around wreaking havoc, egging cars and houses, and worst of all, he was known for beating up homeless drunks for "fun."

The quintessential college douchebag. After dropping out of school, he started working at a local casino and then applied to be a cop but couldn't move forward because he was colorblind. In 1982, when he was twenty-six, his parents encouraged him to obtain his embalming license so he, too, could join the family biz. This would go on to be a huge mistake.

He himself didn't love the idea but knew there was a great deal of money to be made. After obtaining his license, he started his own cremation company called Coastal Cremations Inc., and because he was like a funerary nepo baby, he was able to use two of the crematory furnaces that his family owned to start the business. His idea was to charge less than half of what others were offering at the time, but this wasn't to provide relief to grieving families, this was part of a marketing ploy to do as much business as possible. And you gotta wonder, how was this possible? Many didn't question it because he was pulling in the numbers, by 1985 providing more than eight thousand cremation services a year out of a crematorium that the family owned in neighboring Altadena. Day and night things were a-cookin' in there; the ovens allegedly ran for eighteen hours a day.

So again, how were they able to pull this off? Well, that's why we're writing about it here. David was cremating in . . . bulk. Bulk cremations. That's right, he had his guys cremating anywhere from five to eighteen bodies *per* furnace. Obviously the biggest question is how could they possibly know whose ashes were whose? Well they couldn't! He instructed his workers to bag three and a half to five pounds of the mixed ashes for women, and five to seven pounds for men and would give these to the families. Can you believe it?! *Oh*, that's not all—in November 1986, the crematorium burnt down because two employees attempted to break the company record by putting NINETEEN BODIES in each of the two furnaces. A fire broke out because the chimney was clogged and burnt it the fuck down.

Luckily for David, he had already secretly purchased another crematorium seventy miles away, in Hesperia, but he wasn't running it as a funeral home. No, no, David was operating it as a "ceramics factory." He did this so that he could purchase these massive diesel kilns used for baking pottery when really he was using them for cremation. This went on until December 23, 1986, when somebody who lived nearby had had enough of the constant smoke in the air and decided to alert authorities. When the crematorium was raided, reports were that the soles of the inspector's shoes stuck to the floors, which were slick with human fluids. And when they pried open one of the hinged doors of Sconce's kilns, the remains of a foot fell out, engulfed in flames.

The most disgusting part is that the bulk cremations were just *part* of the scam. He was pulling gold teeth and selling the gold to his pal who was a jeweler, allegedly raking in an additional $6,000 a month from this alone! He was selling brains—136 sold in total that they know of—skin tissue, hearts, and lungs to medical schools, just fucked! We read one article about this case on *Cracked* and they said,

> He employed many of his old football buddies as muscle, not just to transport and handle the dead bodies, but also to intimidate funeral home directors into doing business with Coastal Cremations and scare or beat the crap out of anyone who could potentially expose their misdeeds. For years, thousands of bereaved family members dealing with funeral plans for their loved ones had no idea that a Scorsese movie was taking place behind the scenes. . . .
>
> In February of 1985, Sconce sent another one of his thugs, this time a 245-pound ex–football player, to beat up a rival crematorium owner Timothy Waters, who had been threatening to spill all of the tea on Sconce's operation. Two months later, Waters was dead, presumably of

a heart attack. The autopsy report found traces of the heart medication digoxin in his bloodstream, only Waters was not on any heart medication.

In May 1988, David Sconce, Jerry Sconce, and Laurieanne Lamb Sconce were together charged with sixty-seven felony and misdemeanor counts. This included, the *Los Angeles Times* reported, "illegally harvesting eyes, hearts, lungs, and brains for sale to a scientific supply company, conducting mass cremations, falsifying death certificates, and embezzling funeral trust account funds." David was also charged separately with "assaulting three morticians who voiced suspicions about the family's cremation operation."

This all led to a class-action lawsuit filed by the relatives of five thousand deceased people against the Lamb Family Funeral Home and other funeral homes that used its services; the lawsuit was settled out of court in 1992 for $15.4 million.

As the Sconces awaited arraignment, the police made another morbid discovery. In May 1988, a pile of charred bones, teeth, and prosthetic devices was found in the crawl space beneath David Sconce's former rental home in Glendora, where he had lived until early 1987. Furniture salesman Ed Shain, who rented the house after Sconce's departure, discovered the remains while replacing the screen on the crawl space and called the authorities, who then spent two days filling two large boxes full of bones, dentures, bridges, bits of skull, pacemaker wires, and a soda can packed with molars. Sconce had bulldozed the front- and backyards of the house before leaving town, but he hadn't completely covered his tracks.

On September 1, 1989, Sconce was sentenced to a five-year prison term after pleading guilty to twenty-one charges, including mutilating corpses, conducting mass cremations, and hiring hit men to attack the competing morticians Ron Hast, his partner Stephen Nimz, and Timothy Waters. In 1990, while Sconce was still in prison, new charges were brought against him for Waters's death, but the case was ultimately dismissed after three separate toxicologists, including Dr. Fredric Rieders—who later testified in the O. J. Simpson case—could not agree if there was oleander poison in Waters's blood. Due to various plea deals, Sconce would ultimately serve only two and a half years of his sentence. He was released in 1991.

In April 1992, five years after their arrest, Laurieanne and Jerry Sconce, now fifty-five and fifty-eight, retired and living penniless in Arizona, walked through the doors of the Pasadena Superior Court to stand trial for their part in the conspiracy—in particular, the forging of authorization forms to remove organs from the dead. "These acts were done by their son, David," began Laurieanne's defense attorney in his opening statement, describing the mass cremations and stealing of gold teeth. "It was done without their permission or knowledge. It's resulted in a great tragedy for them, for a third-generation business, and for the families of the deceased." During the questioning, the couple threw their son under the bus, blaming him for the cremation conspiracy. Thirty-six charges had already been dismissed before the trial, and the couple was acquitted of three charges, and a mistrial was declared for the other six. But two years later, thirty-four of the original charges were reinstated by a state appellate court, and in 1995, the Sconces were convicted with ten counts between them of "unlawfully authorizing the removal of eyes, hearts, lungs, and brains from bodies prior to cremation," reported the *Los Angeles Times*. They were each sentenced to three years and eight months in prison.

As for David Sconce, he would return again and again to court, with new charges and new parole violations. In 1994, he was found guilty of selling fake bus tickets in Arizona. In 1997, Sconce pleaded guilty to a 1989 charge of soliciting a hitman to murder a potential buyer of a rival funeral home and was given the unusual sentence of lifetime probation in California. He violated this probation by moving to Montana without permission in 2006, and again by stealing a neighbor's rifle in 2012. Charged with four felonies, he was extradited to California and sentenced to twenty-five years to life. He remained incarcerated at Mule Creek State Prison in Ione, California, and was released on parole in 2023.

5

THE LAST WORD

Obituaries are one of those things you never really think about until you have to, or maybe you're just like us and spent your childhoods handing off the "funnies" to your siblings so you could scour homages to the deceased in peace. Death is the one thing we can all expect, while simultaneously being the biggest mystery to those of us still living. Writing a final farewell to a loved one can feel like there's so much pressure behind it. Like, how on earth am I going to encapsulate this wonderful person in a few sentences? Or, if you have the budget for it, a few paragraphs. It can definitely feel like a daunting task.

But you know what's worse than writing an obituary for somebody you loved? Writing one for somebody you kinda hated. Obituaries are nothing new, in fact some of the first "death notices" date all the way back to 59 BCE. Of course, they looked a little different back then. It was the Romans who first began releasing the Acta Diurna, Latin for "daily proceedings." Essentially this was their version of a daily newspaper posted for the public to see. This was centuries before printing presses, so they relied on the Flintstones-esque practice of carving their announcements into literal slabs of stone, sometimes sheets of metal when available. Wild, right?! In 1436, German goldsmith Johannes Guten-berg invented one of the first printing press apparatuses, and with that came what's referred to as the "Printing Revolu-tion." As printing became more accessible, newspapers went from being an average of three to four pages to as long as forty pages as printing machinery continued to advance. By 1886, a new invention called the linotype was released, which made it way easier to print the small type we're used to seeing in newspapers now. With longer prints and smaller type, there was more space to fill, and more room for obituaries. The earliest form of obituaries were referred to as "death notices," and they're exactly what they sound like: a notice sent out to announce the death of a local. It was the only way to spread the message in the days before social media and cell phones.

Death notices included the need-to-knows about the de-ceased person: legal name, date of birth, date of death, some-times funeral service details, where they lived, birthplace . . . you get the gist. Very matter-of-fact, which honestly makes them pretty interesting to skim through because it wasn't uncommon for death notices to include details about how somebody passed. For example, Paulus Gutermuth's obituary read, "He died at the age of 82 years, 1 month and 2 days, on

24 January 1898. . . . He died of Pneumonia." It wasn't until the late 1900s that obituaries for "common folk" started to rise in popularity, detailing lives well lived and becoming those "short biographies" that switched the focus from the person's death to how they lived. It's not uncommon to see an almost Wikipedia-style obituary in the papers, think: early life, career, personal life, later life, and death. You'll see important dates scattered throughout such as weddings, the birth of a child, even their employment history.

But what makes a good obituary? To us it's when you walk away from reading it feeling like you knew the person, for better or for worse. Bad obituaries can go on forever about the person's life and you still walk away without any feel for their personality. The best ones can be two words and even then make you think, *Oh yeah, that was perfect.* Like one of our favorites from the *OBITCHUARY* vault, for a man named Douglas Legler, who passed away in June 2015. According to his daughter, Doug repeatedly asked that when he died, his obituary would consist of only two words: "Doug died." She was happy to oblige, and his obituary was printed as such.

Obituaries of the scathing variety are really what inspired our ventures into the world of the macabre. I mean hello . . . it's why we put the *bitch* in *OBITCHUARY*! Yes they're hilarious, in an absurd morbid way, but really it's the shock factor. Who would have thought that such a thing existed, and what would prompt somebody to write one? Well, as it turns out, there's a variety of reasons. The truth of the matter is, some people just plain suck. We can all probably name at least one person in our lives worthy of some petty last words.

A lot of people choose to live their lives based on their conditioning. Perhaps you believe in hell and want to ensure your good deed prevents you from a lifetime of despair or after-lifetime of despair? You get the picture. Or maybe you just believe in the law of attraction, you receive what you put out into the universe.

Regardless of where your moral compass originates, we can all agree we'd probably be spinning in our coffins if we received a 1-star Yelp review via our obituary! So perhaps it should serve as a warning: be kind, do good, and try not to be a total dick or else you might just be leaving your legacy in the hands of an angry relative.

Let's not forget, obituaries are costly, so if somebody is going the extra mile to drop $$$ on a final *fuck you*, you might just deserve it. Does everybody who has received a scathing obituary deserve it? Well, there's no way to be certain. Sometimes quite the opposite will occur, where a gloating obituary will attempt to cover up the life of a monster . . . like Michael Haight.

On January 4, 2023, Enoch, Utah, police discovered a gruesome scene at the home of Michael and Tausha Haight. In the home were eight bodies, all shot to death, including the body of Michael Haight, who had died by suicide after murdering his entire family.

As a further tragedy to his wife and children, an unnamed person(s) wrote a disturbing obituary, noting, "Michael made it a point to spend quality time with each and every one of his children. Michael enjoyed making memories with the family."

The obit noted the births but not the deaths of each of his children, whom he murdered. It painted a picture of a family man, a churchgoer, a doting husband who loved spending time with his family, whom again—he brutally killed. The obit even claimed, "He excelled at everything he did." Eew.

What this obituary fails to mention is that forty-two-year-old Michael murdered his entire family. His wife, Tausha Haight, forty; three daughters, seventeen, twelve, and seven; and two sons, aged seven and four; *and* he also killed his mother-in-law, Gail Earl, seventy-eight. If ever someone deserved a scathing obituary, here he is.

Obituaries are meant for the living, but this one was super disrespectful to the victims, in our opinion. The obituary has since been pulled by its original publisher, Utah's *The Spectrum* . . . but, babe, it's 2023, and the screenshots are everywhere. Not cool.

On a lighter note, "A plus-sized Jewish lady redneck died in El Paso on Saturday." Could you imagine those being the first words of your obituary? They were for Renay Corren. Described by her son as "the bawdy, fertile, redheaded matriarch," this is how the world read that Renay had died, or in the obituary's words, "she had kicked it."

At first you think you're reading a roast. Her son makes jabs at Mom's gambling, bankruptcy, multiple divorces, and other things you generally wouldn't want to be remembered for. But then, in the end, you see it was the shared sense of humor between mother and son, which connected them in life and now in death.

There will be much mourning in the many glamorous locales she went bankrupt in: McKeesport, PA, Renay's birthplace and where she first fell in love with ham, and atheism; Fayetteville and Kill Devil Hills, NC, where Renay's dreams, credit rating, and marriage are all buried. . . .

Here's what Renay was great at: dyeing her red roots, weekly manicures, dirty jokes, pier fishing, rolling joints, and buying dirty magazines. She said she read them for the articles.

I mean, c'mon, does it get better than that? We just know Renay would be rolling over with laughter . . . and as far as "reading" for the "articles," we say . . . Sure, Renay, us too!

The obituary goes on: "We thought Renay could not be killed. God knows, people tried. A lot. Renay has been toying with death for a decades [*sic*], but always beating it and running off in her silver Chevy Nova. Covid couldn't kill Renay. Neither could pneumonia twice, infections, blood clots, bad feet, breast cancer twice, two mastectomies, two recessions, multiple bankruptcies, marriage to a philandering Sergeant Major, divorce in the 70's, six kids, one cesarean, a few abortions from the Quietly Famous Abortionist of Spring Lake, NC, or an affair with Larry King in the 60's."

And then, Renay's son concludes, "Please think of the brightly-frocked, frivolous, funny and smart Jewish redhead who is about to grift you, tell you a filthy joke, and for Larry King's sake: LAUGH. Bye, Mommy. We loved you to bits."

This obit was first published in the *Fayetteville Observer* in 2021 and goes in the Obituary Hall of Fame because the hilarious details give readers such a good look at what a wild and vivacious gal Renay was.

It's all well and good when you're writing an obituary, even one with a fair amount of bitchiness, for someone you loved, but what happens when you're stuck writing an obituary for someone you hated? While most will opt to keep things short and to the point, others have opted to pen what we call a scathing obituary. Sure there's the whole, "if you don't have anything nice to say, say nothing" logic. But where's the fun in that? We've seen obituaries written for literal murderers that make the deceased person sound like a saint, as mentioned, but these next obituaries are examples of what happens when people decide to keep it real . . . perhaps too real. Kathleen Dehmlow has entered the chat.

Kathleen Dehmlow of Springfield, Minnesota, passed away on May 31, 2018. She received one of the most scathing obituaries we've ever read. It turns out she was married in 1957 and had two children, Gina and Jay. Sometime after that, she got pregnant by her husband's brother (!) and ditched the fam for California. Gina and Jay were raised by their grandparents, and they were none too pleased about it. Kathleen's obit read, "She will not be missed by Gina and Jay, and they understand that this world is a better place without her."

DAMN.

Kathleen's obituary went viral upon its release in the *Redwood Falls Gazette* in 2018, which was later taken down after an onslaught of commenters complained about the harsh obit. Gina and Jay spoke out later on about why they decided to publish the piece, and for them it appears to come down to wanting to have the last word.

Not all scandalous obituaries leave an everlasting bad mark on a name. In 1888, Alfred Nobel's brother Ludvig Nobel passed away, but the French newspaper accidentally published an obituary for Alfred—oopsy daisy. The obit referred to Alfred as the "merchant of death" due to his invention of dynamite, which was then being used in warfare. Imagine not only was your obituary mistakenly printed but also . . . they dogged you in it? This incident reportedly had a profound impact on Alfred Nobel, leading him to establish the Nobel Prizes in order to leave a more positive legacy. Mission accomplished. We didn't even know about the dynamite.

ACTUAL (OR LEGENDARY) LAST WORDS

Obits are often referred to as "the last word." But what about the actual very last word? Have you ever wondered what your last words would be? What would you say? Would you even have time to say it?

We hope that whatever our last words are, they're good and not something basic like "Oh shit!" Or something traumatic like that. We looked up some famous people and what they said on their deathbeds and came across a bunch of interesting tidbits. So let's start with:

Nostradamus: The French astrologer and physician predicted, "Tomorrow, at sunrise, I shall no longer be here." He was right.

Marie Antoinette: The unpopular queen of France before the French Revolution was sentenced to execution. She stepped on her executioner's foot on her way to the guillotine, uttering her final words, "Pardon me, sir. I did not do it on purpose."

Gustav Mahler: The famous Austro-Bohemian romantic composer died in bed conducting an imaginary orchestra. His last word was "Mozart!"

Wolfgang Amadeus Mozart: Arguably one of the most popular classical composers, said, "The taste of death is upon my lips, I feel something that is not of this earth." He passed shortly after.

Jean-Philippe Rameau: The influential French composer of the eighteenth century had a priest sing to him while he was on his deathbed. Jean-Philippe did *not* like it. He said, "What the devil do you mean to sing to me, priest? You are out of tune." Shame on that priest for being out of tune!

Elvis Presley: The "King of Rock 'n' Roll" is thought to have uttered, "I'm going to the bathroom to read" as his last words. He did say that to his fiancée, Ginger, but the last thing he actually said was "I won't," because she told him not

*I'm going to the
bathroom to read.
-Elvis*

to fall asleep on the toilet. She later found him on the bathroom floor unresponsive.

Frank Sinatra: "Ol' Blue Eyes," one of the most popular singers/actors of the twentieth century, said "I'm losing," to his wife, Barbara, and his manager, Tony.

George Orwell: The English novelist's last written words were, "At 50, everyone has the face he deserves." He died at age forty-six.

Johnny Ace: The famous American R&B singer died in 1954 while playing with a pistol during a break in his concert set. Apparently he was waving it around, even at his girlfriend and friends in the room. He assured everyone that it wasn't loaded. His last words were, "I'll show you that it won't shoot." He shot himself in the head.

Richard Feynman: The physicist and Nobel Prize winner died of cancer in Los Angeles in 1988. His last words? "This dying is boring."

Humphrey Bogart: Old Hollywood's acting icon said, "Goodbye, kid. Hurry back." Bogart was suffering from esophageal cancer and spoke those words to his wife, Lauren Bacall, because she had to leave his bedside to pick up their kids.

Ernest Hemingway: The American novelist died from a self-inflicted gunshot. Before he took his life, he told his wife, Mary, "Goodnight, my kitten."

Groucho Marx: One of the legendary Marx brothers, the comedian and actor was hospitalized after a battle with pneumonia. His last words were "This is no way to live!"

Chico Marx: The eldest Marx brother said to his wife, "Remember, honey, don't forget what I told you. Put in my coffin a deck of cards, a mashie niblick, and a pretty blonde."

Winston Churchill: The last words of the prime minister of Great Britain in the 1940s and '50s were "I'm bored with it all." Us too!

Truman Capote: The American author and *Breakfast at Tiffany's* writer repeated, "Mama—Mama—Mama" on his deathbed.

I'm going away tonight! -James Brown

James Brown: The "Godfather of Soul" and hardest-working man in show business said, "I'm going away tonight."

Steve Jobs: The cofounder of Apple said, "Oh wow. Oh wow. Oh wow," according to his sister Mona.

Princess Diana: The Princess of Wales is reported to have said, "My God. What happened?" to a firefighter after she was in a terrible car crash caused by paparazzi and her driver, who was reportedly under the influence. She survived only a few hours after the crash at a nearby hospital. It took twenty years for the French firefighter on the scene to reveal her last words. It's possible she had further words with her children over the phone, but these have never been revealed.

Lucille Ball: One of our personal favorite actors and comedians said, "My Florida water," which was in response to being asked if there was anything she wanted (her favorite perfume).

Desi Arnaz: Lucille Ball's ex-husband and co-star of *I Love Lucy* passed away before her. Two days before his death, he had one last conversation with her. His final words to her: "I love you too, honey. Good luck with your show."

Charlie Chaplin: The famous silent film star said, "Why not? After all, it belongs to him." This was in response to a priest reading him his rites, specifically the part "may the Lord have mercy on your soul."

Stan Laurel: The comedian and actor best known for Laurel and Hardy, said to his nurse, "I'd rather be skiing!"

Steve Irwin: The famous "Crocodile Hunter" was killed by a stingray in Australia in 2004. His cameraman said, "He calmly looked up at me and said, 'I'm dying.' And that was the last thing he said. . . . Those were his final words."

John Lennon: The Beatles front man was murdered by gunshot in the eighties. He is reported to have said, "Yes," after being asked by an EMT in the ambulance if he was John Lennon. However, that is still up for debate. Most people agree that his real last words were "I'm shot!"

Joe DiMaggio: The baseball legend and Marilyn Monroe's former husband uttered, "I'll finally get to see Marilyn," before he passed away in 1999. He and Marilyn were only married for 274 days, but it is said that she is the only woman he's ever truly loved. They remained friends until her death in 1962. He never remarried.

Debbie Reynolds: The famous Hollywood actress, best known for her breakout role in the 1952 film *Singin' in the Rain* with Gene Kelly, passed away the day after the death of her daughter, actress Carrie Fisher. Debbie's son said her last words were, "I want to be with Carrie."

Ted Bundy: The American serial killer said, "I'd like you to give my love to my family and friends," before being executed for murder.

Edward H. Rulloff: The Canadian-born American-convicted murderer said, "I'd like to be in hell in time for dinner." He was the last person to be hanged in the state of New York.

Joan Crawford: One of the most famous stars of the 1930s and '40s yelled, "Damn it! Don't you dare ask God to help me," on her deathbed. These were her last words in response to her housekeeper praying over her.

*Don't you dare ask
God to help me!
- Joan Crawford*

OBITUARY

THEODORE HOWARD

As you're probably beginning to sense, people don't always hold back when it comes to penning an obituary—or make an attempt at highlighting themselves. Case in point, the ex-wife and mother to the children of Theodore Howard, who ensured everyone reading his obit knew she was his number one ride-or-die.

It started out simple enough: *Home-going celebration for Theodore*

Howard. The sun rised December 24, 1946, but when the sun set Theodore was gone. He passed away at 7 PM on April 2, 2005, he was born in Bonita Louisiana to the reunion of his beautiful mother Annette Howard and his mean father Abner Conway. All the usual deets but then things went awry in a perhaps too honest unfolding.

This is where he met and fell in love with his wife Peewee later they moved to Compton California where she's bared his children. She's a damn good mother who was faithful and devoted to her man "too devoted" she got a wake up call they parted she never went back but she never stop caring and doing good things for him like now he didn't have insurance policy but PV made it possible she made sure he is having a good proper burial service right now she will help anyone long as they are not playing games.

You gotta appreciate the honesty . . . . if anything it's pretty entertaining.

The author continued on with their unabashed truth-telling, adding: *Theodore was a good man a jealous man who needed anger management classes jealous over his woman he didn't want any other man speaking or buying anything for his woman Percy Sledge sums it up with his song when a Man loves a woman can't keep my mind on nothing else. The first time meeting Theodore you probably wouldn't like him because of his choice of words in the harshness of his tone of voice. He reminds me af BJ that TV series with Mr. T what are you looking at for. But to know him is to love him he was a hard-working man . . .*

6

COFFIN CONFESSIONS

He never liked you!

Job Opportunity
COFFIN CONFESSOR

Description: Carry out the after-death wishes of clients once deceased. Under zero supervision, you will deliver devastating or shocking news, share critical information, and reveal long-held secrets. Must be comfortable destroying private evidence or personal matters of clients, interrupting eulogies, or performing other tasks as requested by client.
Benefits: Provide closure for clients and possibly their loved ones.
Qualifications: Must be discreet. Must have thick skin.

This might sound like a joke but it's a *legit job*. Coffin confessors have been around for years, helping clients reveal their secrets or deliver messages after their death. A coffin confessor is an individual who is hired to attend a funeral or memorial service and reveal secrets, confessions, or important messages on behalf of the deceased. The role is intended to bring closure, resolve conflicts, or share revelations. This might be revealing hidden secrets, confessing to past wrongdoings, or disclosing things individuals didn't want to deal with in life. It's like a final act of truth-telling from the recently deceased.

Imagine a coffin confessor stepping up during a somber funeral, captivating the attendees with shocking revelations or heartwarming messages. It's like a plot twist in the grand theater of life. Because no matter the message, the confessor's role is to ensure that the wishes of the departed are fulfilled, allowing them to have their final say, even if it's from six feet under.

It's important to note that coffin confessors are not frequently used. The service is typically arranged in advance by the deceased or their loved ones who are aware of the hidden secrets or messages to be shared. It adds a unique and sometimes controversial element to the funeral proceedings, as it unveils a side of the deceased that may have been unknown or hidden during their lifetime.

Before coffin confessors came around, we're talking pre-seventeenth century here, there were sin-eaters! A sin-eater is a character deeply rooted in certain cultural traditions, particularly in British and Welsh folklore. The concept of a sin-eater revolves around a person who takes on the sins or transgressions of the deceased by means of a ritualistic act.

Traditionally, when someone passed away, it was believed that their sins could linger and affect their journey into the afterlife. To prevent this, a sin-eater would be called upon to absorb the sins of the departed. The sin-eater would partake in a ceremony where they would symbolically consume food or drink that represented the sins of the deceased. Sometimes they did this by eating bread left on the corpse's chest or face. Other times, they ate food that had merely been held over the dead body.

By taking on this role, the sin-eater was thought to absolve the departed of their sins and carry the burden on their own conscience. It was believed that the sins transferred to the sin-eater would release the deceased from the weight of their transgressions, allowing them a better chance of reaching a peaceful rest in the afterlife.

In all cases, sin-eaters were paid next to nothing for their service. And despite "removing" sins from dead people—and taking them on themselves—they were universally reviled. Sin-eaters were often outcasts or individuals on the fringes of society, as their role was seen as both necessary and taboo. They would perform their duties in solemn and secretive ceremonies, typically held at the deceased person's home or graveside. The act of being a sin-eater was shrouded in mystery and superstition, and it was believed that interacting with them could bring bad luck or spiritual contamination.

Now you're probably thinking, who the hell would sign up to do this? People who needed to eat, folks who didn't have access to meals, and I guess a lot of alcoholics—aside from a free meal they were also sometimes given alcohol in exchange for their services.

The practice began to fade out in the nineteenth century and the last known sin-eater was a man named Richard Munslow, who wasn't even down on his luck, he was a farmer who performed the ritual after losing three of his children because he wanted them to die pure. After his death in 1906, the practice apparently came to a halt.

What type of sins were these eaters absolving? Who knows. The only sins we know of for sure were those revealed by the sinners themselves, often divulged on their way out. People have revealed crazy things on their deathbed, often shedding light on unresolved mysteries or admitting to past actions with far-fetching consequences. Here's one example . . .

OBITUARY

VAL PATTERSON

Val Patterson's obit was published by the *Salt Lake Tribune* on July 15, 2012. This guy did not want to leave this earth with a single thread undone. He wrote his own obituary, where he made confessions about certain aspects of his life. He admitted that he did not possess a legitimate PhD from the University of Utah due to a records mix-up. Additionally, he confessed to stealing a safe from a motel and (worst of all) being banned from SeaWorld and Disneyland. Not Disneyland!

Val was born in 1953 and unfortunately passed from throat cancer in 2012. He expressed in his obituary that when he was young he smoked cigarettes, knowing they were bad for him, but felt invincible because of his age and deeply regrets it.

He had quite an interesting life journey, attending six different grade schools before moving on to Churchill, Skyline, and the University of Utah. He really enjoyed school and had a deep love for Salt Lake City, the mountains, and the state of Utah.

Val was a true scientist at heart, with a wide range of interests and skills. He was into electronics, chemistry, physics, auto mechanics, woodworking, art, invention, and even had a knack for business. On top of that, he had a great sense of humor and was known for his ribald comedy. He was also a loving husband, brother, son, and a dedicated cat lover. Val expressed in his obit:

It was an honor for me to be friends with some truly great people. I thank you. I've had great joy living and playing with my dog, my cats and my parrot. But, the one special thing that made my spirit whole, is my long love and friendship with my remarkable wife, my beloved Mary Jane. I loved her more than I have words to express. Every moment spent with my Mary Jane was time spent wisely. Over time, I became one with her, inseparable, happy, fulfilled. I enjoyed one good life. Traveled to every place on earth that I ever wanted to go. Had every job that I wanted to have. Learned all that I wanted to learn. Fixed everything I wanted to fix. Eaten everything I wanted to eat. My life motto was: "Anything for a Laugh". Other mottos were "If you can break it, I can fix it", "Don't apply for a job, create one". I had three requirements for seeking a great job; 1—All glory, 2—Top pay, 3—No work.

Now for the hilarious confessions:

As it turns out, I AM the guy who stole the safe from the Motor View Drive Inn back in June, 1971. I could have left that unsaid, but I wanted to get it off my chest.

Love your honesty, Val!

Also, I really am NOT a PhD. What happened was that the day I went to pay off my college student loan at the U of U, the girl working there put my receipt into the wrong stack, and two weeks later, a PhD diploma came in the mail. I didn't even graduate, I only had about 3 years of college credit. In fact, I never did even learn what the letters "PhD" even stood for. For all of the Electronic Engineers I have worked with, I'm sorry, but you have to admit my designs always worked very well, and were well engineered, and I always made you laugh at work.

When life hands you a PhD, use it, I guess!

Now to that really mean Park Ranger; after all, it was me that rolled those rocks into your geyser and ruined it. I did notice a few years later that you did get Old Faithful working again. To Disneyland—you can now throw away that "Banned for Life" file you have on me, I'm not a problem anymore—and SeaWorld San Diego, too, if you read this.

We wouldn't be caught dead at SeaWorld! Val went on to say:

To the gang: We grew up in the very best time to grow up in the history of America. The best music, muscle cars, cheap gas, fun kegs, buying a car for "a buck a year"—before Salt Lake got ruined by over population and Lake Powell was brand new. TV was boring back then, so we went outside and actually had lives. We always tried to have as much fun as possible without doing harm to anybody—we did a good job at that.

Ending his heartfelt yet hilarious obit, he wrote:

My regret is that I felt invincible when young and smoked cigarettes when I knew they were bad for me. Now, to make it worse, I have robbed my beloved Mary Jane of a decade or more of the two of us growing old together and laughing at all the thousands of simple things that we have come to enjoy and fill our lives with such happy words and moments. My pain is enormous, but it pales in comparison to watching my wife feel my pain as she lovingly cares for and comforts me. I feel such the "thief" now—for stealing so much from her—there is no pill I can take to erase that pain.

If you knew me or not, dear reader, I am happy you got this far into my letter. I speak as a person who had a great life to look back on. My family is following my wishes that I not have a funeral or burial. If you knew me, remember me in your own way. If you want to live forever, then don't stop breathing, like I did.

DEATHBED CONFESSIONS

Not everyone takes everything to the grave. Others opt for the shock and awe of a deathbed confession. Leaving the last words to come from their own lips. Despite the name, deathbed confessions aren't always spilled while cozying up on an actual bed or at the moment of someone's final breath. Nope, they can happen anywhere and anytime, but they always come packed with drama and secrets.

Some religions are big believers in spilling the beans before you head into the afterlife. Imagine you're teetering on the edge of the great beyond, and suddenly you feel the urge to confess your sins, like a divine version of "truth or dare." Some even believe that a good ol' deathbed confession might grant them a few extra precious moments on this earthly plane. It's like bargaining with fate for a bonus

round, hoping that the confession buys you a little extra time. Crafty, huh?

Like us, you might be wondering, can you actually get arrested for a deathbed confession? Well, in the good ol' USA, under the right circumstances, a deathbed confession can hold some serious weight in court. If someone fesses up about a crime they were involved in, and then either passes away or their condition worsens, the law doesn't consider it hearsay. That confession can be used as evidence in a criminal trial. Whoa, talk about a confession that keeps on giving!

But here's the plot twist of all plot twists: there have been cases where some not-so-brilliant criminals confessed to murder while on their deathbeds, only to miraculously survive! Oopsy daisy indeed. Can you imagine the shock on their faces when they wake up and realize they've spilled the beans without actually getting that one-way ticket to the afterlife? That's a serious case of foot-in-mouth disease right there.

We went deep into the labyrinth of the internet and boy, did it deliver the craziest deathbed confessions, ones that will leave you in awe! And guess who's got the inside scoop on these jaw-dropping tales? The heroic nurses who've witnessed it all, of course. They're like the secret keepers of humanity's final moments.

One nurse wrote about a ninety-year-old man who dropped a bombshell confession while on his deathbed. This fella admitted that while he was away on business, he actually started another family! Can you imagine the audacity? And guess what? He lived another two years, probably savoring the tangled web he had woven.

Then there's the heart-wrenching story of a World War II veteran battling dementia. He would repeatedly mutter the number twenty-two, leaving his family clueless about its meaning. But just when you thought the mystery couldn't get any deeper, his mental fog cleared up like magic the day before he passed away. Suddenly, he started telling the staff, "Twenty-two men. I killed twenty-two men over there." Can you imagine carrying that heavy burden for over fifty years? It's enough to make your heart ache for the poor soul.

Now, let's dive into a tale that could rival the wildest crime novels. It involves James Brewer, a man living in Tennessee back in 1977. Convinced that his neighbor Jimmy Carroll was trying to seduce his beloved wife, Dorothy, James flew into a jealous rage and shot him, causing Carroll's untimely demise. But no one ever knew who killed Jimmy Carroll—at least not until James himself was close to death. In a desperate bid to cleanse his soul before departing this earthly realm, James confessed to the murder when he suffered a stroke in 2009. But here's the twist—the dude didn't actually die! Oh no, he survived, forcing James and Dorothy to come out of hiding and surrender themselves back in Tennessee. Talk about a twist of fate.

On the same note, there was an eighty-six-year-old woman on her deathbed, surrounded by a bunch of crosses in her room. When the nurses kindly asked her to remove them due to medical concerns, she defiantly insisted they all stay put. And why, you might ask? Because she claimed that each cross represented a soul she had taken. Fourteen crosses for fourteen departed souls. Now, if her story holds true, that's one mysterious lady with a surprising secret.

Lastly, one of our favorite confessions that will make you question reality. Loch Ness monster sightings have been going on for centuries, but the most famous photographic evidence supposedly came from the 1930s. Colonel Robert Wilson, a British surgeon, claimed to have captured the elusive Nessie in the iconic "Surgeon's Photo." For decades, people believed it was solid proof of the monster's existence. But in a shocking turn of events, Christian Spurling confessed on his deathbed that he and his stepfather, along with Wilson, had staged the whole thing. It turns out they used a toy submarine with a fake animal head attached to create the infamous snapshot. The Loch Ness monster was left high and dry, folks!

So there you have it, the tantalizing world of deathbed confessions. From secret sins to sudden conversions and even courtroom drama, these final admissions remind us that life is a whirlwind of surprises, even in our final moments. So, if you find yourself on your deathbed one day, make sure to choose your words wisely. And who knows, you might just leave behind a legacy that keeps the rumor mill churning for years to come. Cheers to secrets, surprises, and the audacity of spilling the tea when it matters most!

While some opt to confess, others take it all to the grave; however, the things they kept to themselves don't necessarily die with them. For example, Guillermo del Castillo, a.k.a. Chubby, was exposed as a cheater when his mistress posted an obituary for him directly under the one his family had written. His wife wrote, "Your wife Graciela and your son Pablo and Maria Laura say goodbye with pain." And his mistress added, "My dear Chubby, my Guille . . . Thanks for these five years of happiness. Your love forever, Susana."

And as if that's not bad enough, there's more. . . .

OBITUARY

CARLTON MCLEOD

Carlton had a big secret and that secret was exposed on June 11, 2017, when he was honored with not one but two obituaries by two women in Jamaica's *The Gleaner.* They even used the same photo! When he died in 2016, the first memoir was from his known family. It read:

Gone & it seems as if it was yesterday, memoires of your love and kindness and caring heart lingers although you are no longer with us, you will always be in our hearts an will not be forgotten. Sadly, missed by: wife Ivy, children Carwin & Jamielle, sister Jean, other relatives and friends.

Directly below it was the second obituary, this from a woman named Paulette, who used a nickname for McLeod. She wrote:

Mcleod-Carlton Lloyd "Mikey"—in loving memory of a dear one, who departed this life on the 10th of June 2016. One sad year. Sadly missed by: son Hugh and dear friend Paulette.

Record scratch. That's right . . . Carlton had a secret son with another woman.

LIVING FUNERALS

For those who want to test-run their funeral before revealing all, there's always a living funeral. And it's exactly as it sounds.

Ever wondered why people save all the nice words for when someone's already six feet under? It's a bit baffling, isn't it? But guess what? Now you can flip the script and take matters into your own hands! We're talking about the mind-blowing concept of hosting your own funeral while you're still alive!

We have to say, we're absolutely smitten with this idea—it's like throwing the party of a lifetime where you get to be the guest of honor! Can you imagine anything more epic than celebrating your life in real time, surrounded by the people who matter most to you?

Let's take a trip to the Land of the Rising Sun, Japan, where this trend took off in the 1990s. They call it seizensō (pronounced *see-zen-so*), and it's an absolute game-changer. Instead of burdening your loved ones with the task of planning and paying for a funeral after you're gone, you take the reins while you're still kicking! You get to plan everything just the way you want it, and yes, foot the bill, too. It's a win-win situation, don't you think?

But here's the thing, friends. Living funerals aren't just for the elderly who want to lighten the load on their loved ones. Oh, no, they're so much more than that! They can be held for a multitude of reasons. Imagine throwing a living funeral on a milestone birthday, like a party that celebrates the journey of your life thus far. Or perhaps when faced with a terminal illness diagnosis, you can choose to embrace the opportunity to gather your loved ones, laugh, cry, and make memories while you still can. It's a chance to break free from the confines of tradition and seize the opportunity to celebrate your life while you're still here to enjoy it. Whether it's a grand extravaganza or an intimate gathering, hosting your own funeral can be a powerful and transformative experience. So, why wait until it's too late to hear all the kind words and bask in the love? Throw that party of a lifetime, and make sure you're there to witness the magic firsthand!

In South Korea, living funerals are looked at as more of a mental awareness and wellness activity, which we actually really love. Here many people take part in living funerals as a pursuit of emotional well-being. They've coined these unique events as "Well Dying," and in our opinion, they're nothing short of extraordinary.

The Hyowon Healing Center in Seoul, a real funeral home, had an ingenious idea back in 2012. They started holding mock funerals, and get this, they've conducted over twenty-five thousand of them since then! Why, you ask? Well, it all comes down to the alarming suicide rates in South Korea. The Hyowon Healing Center wanted to provide an opportunity for individuals to experience death and gain a new perspective on life.

Imagine stepping into a room adorned with a hundred wooden caskets, each accompanied by candles and pictures of people. This is the setting for the mock funeral, where participants get a taste of what death might feel like. It's not about having friends and family celebrate you; rather, it's an immersive experience meant to provoke deep reflection.

Here's how it goes down: as a participant, you arrive at the center, have your picture taken, and don a shroud. Then, you write out a will, contemplating your wishes and reflecting on your mortality. Finally, the moment arrives. You are gently closed inside one of those coffins, where darkness and silence envelop you for a transformative ten minutes.

In a powerful video by NowThis News, the head of the Hyowon Healing Center shares insights into the minds of participants. Jeong Yong-mun explains that many arrive at

the center with their minds made up about life—feeling desperate and contemplating ending it all. However, through
this experience of simulated death, the center aims to reverse
their decisions and help them appreciate life anew. The head
of the center receives heartfelt messages from individuals who
express gratitude for the newfound perspective they gained.

You see, sometimes people need to taste "death" to truly
savor and appreciate life. We often put off reconciling with
loved ones or pursuing our dreams, believing that we have all
the time in the world. But this immersive experience serves as
a poignant reminder that life is finite and every moment is
precious.

But wait, there's more! In a similar vein, there's a program
called "Happy Dying," led by Mr. Kim Ki-ho. The concept
remains much the same: participants have their photo taken
beside a coffin, write their wills and words for their tombstone, and dress in shrouds. However, there's an added di-
mension. According to an article from the *International
Business Times*, a "death master," donned entirely in black,
takes part. This figure, often associated with the Angel of
Death, covers the participants' eyes and ties their wrists together. They are then encouraged to meditate and reflect in
the darkened room for a more extended period of thirty minutes. The experience also prompts contemplation of the consequences that would arise if one were to take their own life,
aiming to guide individuals toward a path of healing and
renewed appreciation for life's blessings.

Whether you find yourself partaking in such a unique experience or simply contemplating the idea of hosting your own living funeral, there's no denying that it's pretty cool! In fact, we've got a few captivating stories to share about individuals who took the reins and held their own living funerals.

Let's look back to the 1930s and delve into the fascinating tale of Felix "Bush" Breazeale from Tennessee. Felix, a bachelor in his seventies, found himself in an intriguing conversation one day with a local businessman who also happened to be the editor of a nearby newspaper. The topic? A majestic walnut tree on Felix's property that caught the businessman's attention. Little did they know, this conversation would lead to something truly extraordinary.

As they chatted about the tree, the discussion turned toward death, dying, and funerals—everything related to the great unknown. It sparked a flame within Felix, igniting a desire to attend his very own funeral, to hear his eulogy and the heartfelt words of others. Inspired by this newfound idea, Felix made the bold decision to cut down that very walnut tree and craft his own coffin. With determination in his heart, he embarked on a five-year journey of planning his own funeral.

Felix's friend, the newspaper editor, was captivated by the story and decided to write about it. Little did they anticipate the immense interest it would garner. Soon, newspapers far and wide picked up the tale, and Felix, in a peculiar twist, became something of a celebrity.

Then, in 1938, the momentous day arrived. Felix, just a few days shy of his seventy-fourth birthday, held his grand funeral. The event drew an astounding crowd of eight thousand people, some of whom camped out for days to secure their spot. Visitors flocked from different states, making the gathering an unforgettable spectacle.

The tiny Cave Creek Baptist Church became the epicenter of the extravaganza. The streets were lined with eager onlookers, while vendors sold snacks to the masses. Two miles of cars stretched along the roads, and photographers captured every moment. Flowers and funeral wreaths adorned the scene, creating an atmosphere of reverence and spectacle.

When the time came, Felix arrived in a hearse, though not in the traditional sense. Instead of resting in his handmade coffin, he chose to sit in the passenger seat up front. Inside the church, he positioned himself right in front of his very own casket, a sight to behold. As the eulogy was delivered, Felix listened intently, savoring each word. When it concluded, he shared his satisfaction, proclaiming, "This will be my only funeral, and I'm mighty well pleased with it. When I die, there won't be another one."

Afterward, Felix shook hands with attendees and even signed autographs, relishing in the unexpected turn of events. He admitted that he never intended for the funeral to become such a grand affair, envisioning a small gathering instead. But once the newspapers caught wind of it, the story took on a life of its own.

In the years that followed, Felix passed away, and true to his word, there was no second funeral. He was laid to rest in the casket he meticulously crafted, a fitting conclusion to his extraordinary journey. From the majestic walnut tree to the throngs of people who celebrated his life, Felix's story reminds us of the profound impact one person can have on the world, even in the face of their own mortality.

Spring forward to 2013, when a remarkable twenty-two-year-old woman named Zeng Jia, a college student in China studying to become an undertaker, made the audacious decision to hold her own funeral.

With a touch of intrigue and a hint of whimsy, Zeng Jia prepared for her unique event. She found herself in a coffin, lying there for hours, accompanied by a Hello Kitty stuffed animal, a symbol of innocence and playfulness. To add an eerily authentic touch, she even hired a makeup artist to transform her appearance into that of a lifeless corpse.

Meanwhile, family and friends gathered around, delivering heartfelt speeches and bidding their farewells. Zeng Jia had embarked on this unconventional journey to gain insight into what people truly thought about her and to hear their goodbyes. Little did she know that this daring experience would leave a lasting impact.

Through this extraordinary act, Zeng Jia discovered a newfound appreciation for life itself. It served as a powerful reminder to cherish the moments, connections, and experiences that make life meaningful. Her own funeral became a transformative event that allowed her to reflect on her own existence and the impact she had on those around her.

Zeng Jia's story is a testament to the unorthodox ways in which we can seek profound understanding and appreciation for life. Her bold step into the realm of her own mortality opened doors to self-discovery and served as an inspiration to all who learned of her remarkable journey.

Lastly, we'll touch on Timothy Dexter. Who sounded like a dick if we're being honest. Timmy was born in 1747 and had a modest upbringing and lacked formal education. However, his unwavering determination and hard work propelled him to remarkable success as a salesman.

But here's the thing—luck seemed to be on Timothy's side. Throughout his endeavors, he stumbled upon fortunate circumstances and made wise moves that propelled his wealth. In the 1790s, he possessed a substantial amount of continental dollar bills, whose value unexpectedly skyrocketed, making him a millionaire. His newfound wealth attracted jealousy from his neighbors, who often dared him to engage in eccentric and outlandish activities. Remarkably, Timothy embraced these challenges, such as sending cats to the Caribbean or shipping coal to a mining town. He had a reputation for being rather unpredictable and eccentric, fueling the perception that he was a bit "nuts."

Timothy's obsession with himself and his grandeur knew

no bounds. He acquired an enormous house adorned with forty statues, including several of himself. He even believed he deserved a noble title, aspiring to become a lord. In his pursuit of self-glorification, he commissioned a tomb that was extravagantly large and gaudy. However, its construction was deemed unsafe, raising questions about the peculiar nature of Timothy's desires.

In a bizarre twist, Timothy orchestrated his own funeral, driven by a desire to gauge people's perception of him. Astonishingly, three thousand individuals showed up to pay their respects. Yet, despite his strict instructions for his wife and children to display intense grief and sorrow, they couldn't help but find humor in the absurdity of the situation. Instead of tears and mournful cries, laughter emanated from their direction, catching the attention of the guests.

To compound the eccentricity of the moment, chaos ensued in the kitchen following the funeral. Timothy, in a fit of anger, resorted to beating his wife with a cane. His reason? Her perceived lack of sorrow and mourning during his orchestrated farewell.

Not long after this unusual display, Timothy Dexter passed away, leaving behind a legacy tinged with controversy. Which is probably what he wanted, right?

PART 3

FUCKED

7

EVIL, AYE

Why do certain people engage in evil activities? It's a complex and multifaceted topic. There isn't a single answer that can fully explain the fucked-up things some people do. Their motivations and actions are usually influenced by a variety of factors, including psychological, social, and environmental aspects. Now, we're no doctors, but we've listed some of the common factors that can contribute to why people might do things like, oh, I don't know—have sex with a corpse. And many other horrifying things you'll read about in this chapter.

Psychological factors: Obviously. There could be underlying issues or personality disorders that contribute to their behavior. Mental health conditions, such as antisocial personality disorder or psychopathy, can diminish empathy and lead to a disregard for others' well-being (whether that person is dead or alive, apparently). Let us be clear: we are in no way saying that everybody who suffers from these mental health qualms is horny for a cadaver, these are just recognized traits and shared disorders in those who have . . . well . . . you know.

Moral disengagement: People will engage in cognitive processes that allow them to justify or morally disengage from their harmful actions. They might convince themselves that what they are doing is acceptable or necessary, distorting their moral compass.

Group dynamics or conformity: Many people can be influenced by group dynamics, where they may conform to the norms and values of a particular group. This conformity can lead them to participate in acts they might not engage in individually, because they seek acceptance, validation, or a sense of belonging.

Lack of empathy: Some people struggle with empathizing with others or understanding the consequences of their actions. They may lack the ability to put themselves in somebody else's shoes, leading to a diminished sense of responsibility for the harm they cause.

We're not giving people a pass by any means for doing horrifying things, just trying to understand why they might want to in the first place. Nothing can excuse or justify their actions. But regardless, we're fascinated with the why, and you are, too. Otherwise you wouldn't be here. Right?

So let's get into some of the evil, horrifying acts people have committed.

NECROPHILIA

Question: What's the strangest, craziest, most horrific thing anybody could ever do with a corpse?
Answer: Have sex with it. Hands down the worst.

According to the Oxford Dictionary, a necrophiliac is a "person who has sexual interest in dead bodies" (pause for gag reflex). Necrophilia is a paraphilia. A paraphilia is basically a condition where you have some very weird and sometimes illegal sexual desires. Equally as bizarre but less gross is ghost sex, also known as spectrophilia.

Necrophilia is derived from the Greek word *phillios*, meaning "love" or "attraction to" and *nekros*, meaning "dead body" or "corpse." It wasn't until 1850 that the term *necrophilia* was really used or even mentioned.

Apparently there are many different types of necrophilia. This shit is wild, y'all! The tamest are the role players who get off on pretending their partner is dead during sexual activity, which—does that even count if the person is actually alive? From there on out it gets weirder. Tactile necrophiliacs are aroused by touching or fondling a corpse, without having actual intercourse. Fetishistic necrophiliacs remove objects from a corpse for sexual purposes, without engaging in intercourse. And then there are full-on exclusives who only have interest in sex with the dead. They cannot perform at all for a living partner. So much for the question, "What does she have that I don't have?" Well, for starters. She's dead.

The cause of necrophilia is still pretty unclear. However, researchers do believe that rejection is a huge motivator. A corpse cannot swipe left, after all. *The Journal of the American Academy of Psychiatry and the Law* says 68 percent of necrophiles were motivated by a "desire for a non-resisting and non-rejecting partner." Twenty-one percent were "motivated by a want for a reunion with a lost partner," and 15 percent were motivated by a "desire for comfort or to overcome feelings of isolation." Any way you hump it, these are sick fucking people.

We'd hate to be famous for a lot of things. Having sexual intercourse with a dead body tops that list. These people thought the reward outweighed that risk:

SERGEANT FRANCOIS REECE BERTRAND A.K.A. "VAMPIRE OF MONTPARNASSE"

In Paris during the 1840s, there were a ton of grave robberies and vandalism at the cemeteries of Père Lachaise and Montparnasse. The guards would occasionally see a figure of a man, and as they would approach he would disappear. The graves and coffins would be found dug up, opened, and if there was a female body, it would be mutilated in some way. Authorities set a booby trap in Montparnasse and the "vampire" was caught and wounded, but escaped. Nobody expected a well-respected model sergeant in the French Army to be their target. The night he was injured in the trap, army superiors saw that he came home wounded. When the topic of local gravediggers spread, they reported Bertrand. He was convicted of necrophilia and only sentenced to one year in prison!

CARL TANZLER

Carl was a radiologic technician during the 1830s in Key West, Florida. He was married with two kids. But as they do, things started to go sideways when he met his side piece, Maria Elena Milagro de Hoyos, a beautiful twenty-two-year-old girl. Carl fell in love with Maria, who soon fell ill with tuberculosis. Carl made it his mission to treat and cure Maria, but just one year later, she died. He was devastated and wanted to make sure she had a place as beautiful as she was to rest. She was buried in a mausoleum in Key West City Cemetery. In 1833, Carl couldn't take it anymore, so he removed her body from the grave and took her home with him (note: he rolled her home in a wagon!).

He created a makeshift medical shed out of an old airplane, and in there, he filled her body with rags to maintain its shape. He kept her skeleton together with piano wire and coat hangers, and replaced her eyes with glass, patching her rotting flesh with silk, wax, and plaster. Tanzler even fashioned a wig for Maria out of her own hair, collected by her mother and gifted to him at her death.

Years later, Maria's sister discovered the body. The authorities were alerted, but due to the statute of limitations on grave robbing, Tanzler didn't face any repercussions. Maria's body was returned to an unmarked grave and—get this—Tanzler moved back in with his estranged wife, who supported him toward the end of his life (despite the fact he was in love with a dead body stuffed with towels living in a shed). But you know, to each their own . . .

KAREN GREENLEE

This twenty-three-year-old apprentice embalmer gave apprentice embalmers a bad name back in 1979. Karen worked at Memorial Lawn in Sacramento, California. On a typical day at work, she was driving a hearse with a body ready for a funeral. Instead of taking it to the funeral, she actually ended up kidnapping it for a while. A joy ride, if you will. During this time, Karen and the corpse had a romantic rendezvous. For Karen, anyway. She was caught after a few days of romping, but necrophilia wasn't illegal in California at the time. Meant for a failed suicide attempt, Karen wrote a confession letter, admitting to having intercourse with almost forty dead bodies.

BODY SNATCHING

In this day and age, when we think about someone's body being SNATCHED, we're like HONEYYYY, YES! We want a snatched summer body! But um, no. No, we do not want to be snatched. Not like this at least.

Body snatching, also known as resurrectionism, refers to the act of unlawfully stealing corpses from burial sites, typically for medical study. Most snatching occurred in the eighteenth and nineteenth centuries, where the demand was high for cadavers for anatomical research and medical education. At the time, studies were advancing but there was limited legal supply of cadavers for schools and research due to strict regulations and a shortage of voluntary donations. So, like most supply-and-demand situations, people looked for a back door. Illegal trade of cadavers emerged, and body snatchers made big on recently buried bodies from graveyards to meet the demand. Early on, grave robbing was merely a misdemeanor, so there wasn't any real risk. It was just real gross.

Central Europe provided ample corpses for medical study. But in the United States, England, and Scotland, medical schools did what they needed to do by sending janitors, students, and medical doctors to dig around in the fresh graves.

The snatchers would shovel at the head of a freshly buried coffin, break the lid, and fish a hook around the deceased neck or armpit, before pulling them from their grave. To ship the bodies, the corpse was folded into a barrel filled with whiskey in order to mask the odor. Once at its destination, the body would be taken away for examination and—put down your latte—the "rotgut" whiskey was sold for consumption as a "stiff drink." True story.

Eventually, the public decided we needed to protect the deceased, and they came up with a variety of tactics to defend the dead. Mort safes, made of iron and stone, were padlocked to the coffins. Nobody was lifting those babies from belowground!

Philip Clover of Columbus, Ohio, developed a device he called the "coffin torpedo" in 1878. In his words, it was a device created to "prevent the unauthorized resurrection of dead bodies." It involved a system of triggers and springs that detonates an explosion of lead balls if the casket lid is opened after burial. Judge Thomas N. Howell invented his revision of the coffin torpedo with the catchy slogan, "Sleep well, sweet angel, let no fears of ghouls disturb thy rest, for above thy shrouded form lies a torpedo, ready to make mincemeat of anyone who attempts to convey you to the pickling vat." Hot damn. Imagine you're just trying to get some cash for gold to get a bump on a Saturday night and—WHAMMY—your meat is minced, babe.

FAMOUSLY ROBBED

Elvis Presley: Three weeks after he died, there was actually a failed grave robbery of the King. Some suspected it was orchestrated by his father, Vernon, to have his son's body re-buried at Graceland.

F. W. Murnau: The skull of the legendary director of *Nosferatu* was stolen from his tomb in Germany in 2015.

Charlie Chaplin: In 1978, two months after his death, Charlie's body was stolen from the grave. The thieves tried to extort his widow, but she said their demands were ridiculous. The thieves were ultimately caught, and Chaplin was returned to his grave.

Groucho Marx: His ashes were stolen from a cemetery in Mission Hills, California. They were later recovered in nearby Burbank.

BRAINS OVER EASY

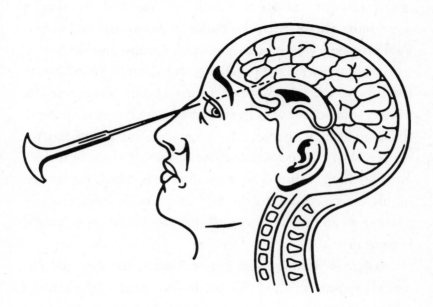

It blows our mind that lobotomies were even a thing, while the procedure itself wasn't considered deadly, it certainly caused the death of many people's spirits. For those not in the know, a lobotomy was a surgical procedure that involved the removal or severing of connections between the prefrontal cortex and other parts of the brain. It was developed in the early twentieth century as a treatment for various mental illnesses and behavioral disorders.

The procedure involved straight-up drilling holes into the skull and using a "specialized instrument," i.e., a freaking ice pick or leukotome (a surgical instrument containing a rotating blade). Yeah. These super trustworthy tools were used to damage neural pathways in the frontal lobes of the brain, supposedly alleviating symptoms associated with schizophrenia, depression, and anxiety disorders. The idea was that by scrambling these areas, the patient's emotional and behavioral problems would be diminished. Because obviously.

Lobotomies gained popularity in the mid-twentieth century due to the mistaken belief they worked. There were, of course, some drawbacks including side effects such as cognitive impairment, personality changes, and motor disturbances. Wait, so people came out of this all kinds of messed up? Shocking, right? The procedure was controversial and highly criticized due to the lack of scientific evidence supporting its efficacy and irreversible nature. But still, people bought in.

Rosemary Kennedy, sibling of Robert Kennedy and former US president John F. Kennedy, was failed by the medical community before she was even born. The doctor had been running late when mother Rose was giving birth and somehow a decision was made to stop the birth from occurring until he got there. To do this, a nurse physically reached inside of Rose's birth canal, and held baby Rosemary in place until the good doctor arrived. This decision resulted in a lack of oxygen to the baby's brain, which would create future damage, resulting in mental deficiency.

At the time, disabilities were not talked about. They were

hidden as much as possible. The Kennedys were looked at as royalty in America, and so they raised Rosemary alongside her siblings, put her through the same school, and completely neglected the fact that she couldn't keep up with the other kids. People started to notice this as she got older, and as a result, when Rosemary was sixteen her parents ended up sending her off to Elmhurst Academy of the Sacred Heart, Providence, Rhode Island, where she was taught separately from the other students.

While she suffered a lot mentally, it has been said she was just a sweetheart, so kind to everybody, even the press. Eventually she was reunited with her family when they moved to England for her father's work. There she attended a Catholic school, where the nuns were super patient with her and she made good progress. Unfortunately, 1940 rolls around and the Nazis stormed Paris, and as a result the Kennedys fled back to the United States where the school system wasn't as kind.

Rosemary allegedly became "difficult" around this time. But in truth, we think she was a very normal twenty-two-year-old girl: having fun, partying with friends, meeting guys at bars, nothing crazy. But to her staunch parents, this was terrifying because her father, Joe, was prepping her brothers to venture into the political sphere.

It has been reported Rose and Joe worried that their daughter's behavior could create a bad reputation not just for herself but for the whole family. So they eagerly searched for a solution that could change her ways. Enter Dr. Walter Freeman, who approached the Kennedys, along with Dr. James

Watts, to tell them all about a new neurological procedure that was all the rage: the lobotomy.

In 1941, at twenty-three years old, Rosemary underwent the procedure. They drilled two holes into her skull and inserted small metal spatulas used to sever the link between the prefrontal cortex and the remainder of the brain, all while Rosemary sat there, reciting poems to her nurses throughout the procedure.

After the lobotomy, she was immediately different, but not for the better. She lost her ability to speak and walk properly, and reportedly had the mental capacity of a two-year-old child. She seemingly vanished from the public eye afterward and was sent to an institution where her family did not visit her for the next twenty years of her life, until Joe had a medical emergency and Rose paid her daughter a visit, during which Rosemary attacked her. Rightfully so if you ask us.

After her father died, Rosemary was brought to visit the Kennedy compounds in Florida and Massachusetts occasionally but continued to reside in an institution. She died in 2005.

We have another famous sibling, Rose Williams, sister of famous playwright Tennessee Williams. When Rose was eighteen, she was sent away by their mother because of her "erratic relationships." She was later committed to a state hospital, where they diagnosed her as a paranoid schizophrenic. In 1943, she received a bilateral prefrontal lobotomy organized by her mother, and we feel like she had a very common response. It wasn't as life altering as Rosemary Kennedy's experience was, but she pretty much became a very flattened-out version of herself. She expressed very little emotion, and was just sort of the shell of the person that she used to be. This caused a huge rift between Tennessee and his mother because he blamed her. Which we would, too, for essentially taking away his sister.

Another one of Dr. Freeman's victims was twelve-year-old Howard Dully. This one breaks our hearts. Howard never struggled mentally, physically, and was overall what you would describe as your typical kid. He was a newspaper delivery boy, and aside from the occasional squabble with his parents, pretty well behaved.

December 1960, just a week before Christmas, the San Jose, California, native was admitted to the hospital to receive a transorbital lobotomy at the urging of his parents because he was "defiant sometimes." How . . . unusual for a child?

Howard was the youngest patient to ever receive a lobotomy from Dr. Freeman, and while he also didn't experience the same reaction as Rosemary Kennedy, life was definitely different for him after the procedure. He spiraled in his teenage years, committing petty crimes, ending up in jail, and then living on the streets. Eventually he got back on track and later wrote about his experience and dropped a startling admission. He told the press that his stepmom threatened to divorce his father if he didn't sign off on the lobotomy because she and the twelve-year-old couldn't see eye to eye.

Can you even imagine? What a piece of shit. Years later, he posted a video on YouTube talking about his experience, and it's just so heavy. They wouldn't tell him why he was in the institution, performed electroshock therapy on him, and generally tortured this kid.

On the flip side, while many of Freeman's patients suffered, some have deemed the procedure to be successful. Such
is the case for Sallie Ionesco, who received the first transorbital or "ice pick" lobotomy in 1946.

The twenty-nine-year-old housewife and mother was
described as violently suicidal. In his office, Freeman admin-
istered electroshock to Ionesco, rendering her unconscious.
He then inserted an ice pick above her eyeball, banged it
through her eye socket into her brain, and then swirled it
around in a sort of eggbeater motion to scramble the neural
connections. The family considered the operation a success
and a blessed relief. She lost some memory function but was
relatively intact, and from there, she led a fairly normal life. . . .
We don't know about you, reader, but how the *hell* was this
allowed? Oh, no big deal, just a little memory function loss,
TRAUMATIC!

Helen Mortensen was Dr. Freeman's last patient. He performed about 3,500 lobotomies in twenty-three states during
his career, of which 2,500 were his ice pick procedure. Helen
first saw Dr. Freeman in 1946 when she was thirty-one years
old. She was one of his very first patients. The transorbital
lobotomy she received appeared to have been effective; however, ten years later, in 1956, she was back for another as she
felt the effects were wearing off. Well, a little over a decade
later, in 1967, she went for her third-freaking-lobotomy. Can
you imagine? It was during this one, the doctor struck a
blood vessel in her brain, completely severing it. And three
days later, Helen was dead.

The hospital revoked Dr. Freeman's surgical practices,
and he retired shortly after.

The moral of the story here, lobotomies are not it. Today, they are considered outdated, thankfully, and ethically reprehensible. So there's that.

BURIED ALIVE!

Imagine waking up to this literal fucking nightmare. . . . You find yourself inside a coffin, six feet under . . . with no pants on. Just kidding about the pants.

There are an insane number of accounts of people who had been buried alive. Some were found still alive, and some sadly died due to lack of oxygen inside the coffin. Now, most of these took place a few centuries ago, so obviously things have changed, e.g., technology, modern medicine, embalming, etc. *But* before we get into being buried alive, we feel it's important to look at the ways in which doctors at the time determined someone was in fact DEAD.

We were fucking losing it reading about all the ways someone was pronounced dead. It is absolutely bonkers. Like we are so grateful for everyone who contributed to science and medicine, and I guess all of these wild experiments because we were able to learn so much and advance so much but holy SHIT. It's SO DUMB.

In getting into some of the ways a doctor would determine someone was dead . . . let's look at the 1800s, when doctors came together and all suggested different things that would make even someone in a coma have some sort of reaction . . . even involuntary actions that could prove that someone was indeed dead.

Galvanism being one of them, where basically electric currents are sent through a body to see if they get a chemical reaction. Maybe it's just us but using electricity to revive a corpse doesn't sound ideal.

Doctors also relied on sticking the corpse's finger in their ear to be able to feel a pulse of some sort. Which is just gross.

Titty twisters and tongue twisters—no, we are not joking. This was a medical thing. Jules Antoine Josat invented the nipple pincher, again—not joking here. Apparently he thought that if anyone were pinched in their nipple, they'd have to wake up.

You're pinching your nipple right now, aren't you?

There was something called a needle flag—where a doctor would stick a long needle with a flag on the end of it directly into the heart. If the flag started moving, the heart was beating. Go science! They were even setting people's noses on fire! In addition to toes, fingers, patches of skin, etc. And even cutting appendages off to inflict enough pain that would sometimes get a person to wake up and live!

Séverin Icard came up with a quite reliable death-test of his own. He found that the subcutaneous injection of a fluorescent solution would cause an animal's skin to turn yellow and eyes to turn green if the subject's circulatory system was still in working order. (There would be no reaction if the subject was dead.) However, this wasn't quite as showy as his written death test. Icard would write the phrase "I am really dead" on a piece of paper in acetate of lead and then place the paper in the alleged corpse's nose. If the acetate encountered sulfur dioxide, a feature of putrefactive gases, then formerly invisible words would become clear on the paper. It was a neat trick, but not a terribly accurate one. Certain dental conditions and tonsillitis could produce the levels of sulfur dioxide necessary to cause the reaction. And an English doctor who tested the process found that only "one out of six corpses affirmed their deaths through this method." Whoopsies.

The next developments to make sure someone wasn't buried prematurely were safety coffins and waiting mortuaries.

A safety coffin, according to the very pragmatic Wikipedia, is "a coffin fitted with a mechanism to prevent premature burial or allow the occupant to signal that they have been buried alive. A large number of designs for safety coffins were patented during the eighteenth and nineteenth centuries and variations on the idea are still available today." Patents for safety coffins first appeared in the late 1800s. These coffins featured a bell, which was attached to a rope you could pull on upon waking up or a handy ladder you could climb up if you were lucky enough to wake up before burial.

Over the next few decades, more innovative features were created, such as mechanisms for allowing airflow into the underground coffin or windows looking in on the body within the coffin. In this thinking, the presumed-deceased could break through the glass if they weren't, ya know, dead. We even found safety coffin patents for ones that had phones, heaters, and even lights so the not-quite-dead could see!

In 1937, there was a man named Angelo Hays who was in a terrible motorcycle accident. He was only nineteen years old and rode his motorcycle into a brick wall, causing a terrible-looking head injury. Long story short, he was pronounced

dead and buried three days later, but his insurance company wanted to investigate further and had his body exhumed. Lo and behold, there was Angelo, alive just in a coma. He fully recovered but went on to invent a security coffin that had a radio transmitter, a refrigerator, oven, and a chemical toilet!

There are a *ton* of stories, especially from that era, of people being accidentally buried alive. . . . Some were exhumed because a family member didn't get to say goodbye, only to pop open the coffin and see a confused person, completely alive. Some bodies have been exhumed, and families found their loved ones dead but in weird positions, as if they were trying to get out, and also scratch marks or indications that they were alive and tried to get out, but died in their coffin. There was even a woman who was saved by her grave robbers. We guess she had on a piece of jewelry they knew about and exhumed her illegally. Imagine the shock when she shot up from the coffin, like get your paws off my bling!

Because of all these oopsy daisies in the eighteenth and nineteenth centuries, people were understandably very afraid of being buried alive. They figured if they were presumed dead, they would still want to wait it out a little. They decided to arrange a stay in the morgue but hold off on funeral and burial arrangements.

This is exactly what a waiting mortuary was for. It was a place used to hold a body and specifically wait and confirm that someone was dead. They were popular in Germany until the 1880s. Newly deceased people would be laid in trays on antiseptic and zinc. Family and friends could come visit them until they started decaying. We guess that was the sign everyone needed to see to call it a day. And if for some reason they did wake up, they had a bell strung on them to make noise to alert staff.

Today, people get buried alive to break records. We read somewhere that the Guinness World Records does not recognize being buried alive, though, because a lot of them have ended tragically. But not for one man . . . Geoff Smith was buried alive for 147 days between 1998 and 1999 in a coffin that he built. He was buried underneath his local pub in the beer garden area. Everything he needed to receive or release was transported through a tube . . . including waste.

OBITUARY

LESLIE RAY CHARPING

This obit, from January 30, 2017, is what you get when someone leads a messy life marked by crappy parenting and overall offensive behavior. Charping didn't bang corpses, but it sounds like he sure did fuck his family over time and time again. Like the body snatchers in this chapter, he was always looking for a quick buck with no regard for who would suffer by his actions. Leslie's passing did not leave behind a positive legacy, so therefore his obituary for the Carnes Funeral Home website, written by his daughter, Shiela Smith, reflects a lack of remorse or condolences regarding his demise.

Leslie Ray "Popeye" Charping was born in Galveston, Texas on November 20, 1942 and passed away January 30, 2017, which was 29 years longer than expected and much longer than he deserved. Leslie battled with cancer in his latter years and lost his battle, ultimately due to being the horses ass he was known for. He leaves behind 2 relieved children; a son Leslie Roy Charping and daughter, Shiela Smith along with six grandchildren and countless other victims including an ex wife, relatives, friends, neighbors, doctors, nurses and random strangers.

Victims!!!!

The author did not hold back when it came to exposing Leslie, from his time in the navy to his off-putting nature-writing:

At a young age, Leslie quickly became a model example of bad parenting combined with mental illness and a complete commitment to drinking, drugs, womanizing and being generally offensive. Leslie enlisted to serve in the Navy, but not so much in a brave & patriotic way but more as part of a plea deal to escape sentencing on criminal charges. While en-listed, Leslie was the Navy boxing champion and went on to sufficiently embarrass his family and country by spending the remainder of his service in the Balboa Mental Health Hospital receiving much needed mental healthcare services.

Yeesh!

Leslie was surprisingly intelligent—we see what ya did there—*however he lacked ambition and motivation to do anything more than being reckless, wasteful, squandering the family savings and fantasizing about get rich quick schemes.*

RIP, Leslie, you would've loved MLMs.

Leslie's hobbies included being abusive to his family, expediting trips to heaven for the beloved family pets and fishing, which he was less skilled with than the previously mentioned.

WHAT?! Not "expediting trips to heaven"!! Oh my GOD.

Leslie's life served no other obvious purpose, he did not contribute to society or serve his community and he possessed no redeeming qualities besides quick whited sarcasm which was amusing during his sober days.

With Leslie's passing he will be missed only for what he never did; being a loving husband, father and good friend. No services will be held, there will be no prayers for eternal peace and no apologizes to the family he tortured. Leslie's remains will be cremated and kept in the barn until "Ray," the family donkey's wood shavings run out. Leslie's passing proves that evil does in fact die and hopefully marks a time of healing and safety for all.

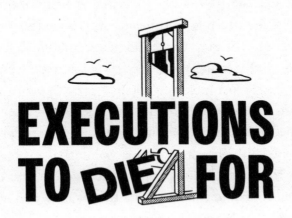

8

EXECUTIONS TO DIE FOR

Do you think the present-day death penalty is outrageous? Honey, we need to talk. Back in the day, things were off the chain. Poisons, torture, posthumous photography. We are obsessed with the medieval and Victorian eras, and after this chapter—you will be, too.

Executions were all the rage, beginning legally in the 1600s. Although they have historically dated much further back to when death penalty laws were first established. We're talking eighteenth century BCE, baby! The public execution was almost like going to a show. People would flock to see the drama and Shakespearean vibes. Regardless of your political affiliation or personal view on capital punishment, the subject is polarizing and has thankfully evolved to a much more humane practice in modern times (in most places). We really want to focus on the sixteenth and seventeenth centuries . . . because they are *wild*! It wasn't until the 1800s that we started reducing the number of crimes punishable by death and even started moving executions inside prison walls. Today, someone could be executed because of a crime they committed that resulted in the death of another person. Back then, the laws were *much* more vague. You could be executed for a multitude of reasons, like stealing food, spreading lies, practicing witchcraft (or simply just looking "witchy"), trading with a Native American, treason, and of course, murder.

In the Victorian era, public executions were part of everyday, normal life. It was a major event that everyone was welcome to attend. Many people would go because they believed that touching the hand of a freshly executed murderer was thought to have magical healing powers. The practice was called "stroking" or the "death stroke." Now, we don't know about you but we would have probably bought into this. And oh my Gawd—there were magical numbers involved! Stroke the hand three, six, nine times to cure ailments like skin tumors, swelling, cysts, goiters, and more! It was believed that this was a cure because of a practice known as transference, where they thought that a criminal's corpse was the perfect receptacle for maladies. It was as if the criminal would receive or relieve the person of those illnesses because they were being transferred from the living to the dead. Why the hand? Because it's closely connected to the brain, obviously. Executions were cool and all, but if there was a beheading—the crowd really went wild! Many people in town believed that the blood was also super healing and could even resolve things like epilepsy.

Have you ever thought about the hooded guy on the other end of an execution? The burly one administering the capital punishment. When we were learning about this topic, we were skeptical about that guy. Naturally. Who was this person? Who would choose to do this as a profession? They sure look ominous and definitely someone we wouldn't want to mess with. But, upon research, their stories were quite sad.

An executioner's role and their daily life obviously looked different from region to region. The era in which one lived changed the scope of their profession, too. In general, the executioner was something of a dichotomy. On one hand, if they were executing a hated criminal, they could be looked at as a hero or a god. But at the same time, they performed a dirty job and were shunned by society due to their unsavory work. They literally lived in separate areas of town, on the outskirts, hidden away from the people who thought less of them.

In some instances, a criminal would be offered the job instead of being executed. But most of the time, the job of executioner was passed down through family. It's kind of like carrying tradition when your grandfather was a cop, your dad was a cop, so there's that expectation you, too, will become a cop. This was referred to as "execution dynasties." This profession was often chosen for people and plagued generations upon generations.

And what's up with that hood? The executioner didn't *always* wear a hood. Some wore normal clothing for the time period. The hoods and masks that we all probably associate with an executioner were worn when there was fear of retaliation from family or friends of the executed. But still, one or both ears were often cut off so the executioners could be easily identified in public. They were also branded . . . on their face! Excuse me?? It turns out they were denied citizenship in the towns where they worked because they were looked down upon. This resulted in them living on the fringes of the village and unable to enter any public establishments . . . even church!

Because they were ostracized from society, if an executioner was lucky enough to find love, their spouse would be subject to the same treatment. Children? The child of an executioner would only associate with other children of executioners and would unfortunately, probably have to follow in their parent's professional footsteps. All that to say, Victorians did not fuck around.

You know who also didn't fuck around? Pirates. Walking the plank will sound like a walk in the park after reading about the execution methods used by the meanest of seamen (giggle, it's okay).

DEATH BY BOILING

Is it hot in here? Trust me when I tell you, you have never been hot until you have been boiled alive! This form of execution was popular in Asia and Europe, dating back to the 1500s. This was also a very public method. Picture a huge cauldron with flames underneath, filled to the brim with liquid. The liquid could be anything from water to oil, tar, fat, tallow, even molten lead! In some instances, the victim was already inside the cauldron as the liquid began to boil, but in most cases they were plunged into the excruciatingly hot liquid. This is another execution method that could some-times take hours to fully take the victim's life. So, what happens when you are turning into human soup? Well, you start to cook! Yes, your skin cooks off first, then your fat, then every organ you have! This includes your brain, people! Eventually, your nerve endings will start to die, and you won't really feel much anymore, or you go into shock and organs start shutting down, whatever happens first.

King Henry VIII actually declared death by boiling the legal form of capital punishment if you were caught poisoning someone. Poisoning fell under the high-treason umbrella. This was after a man named Richard Roose, a chef, was accused of trying to poison Bishop John Fisher, his household, and a few people he had over for dinner. Weirdly enough, the bishop did not eat any of the poisoned food, but allegedly two visitors did and died. Bishop John had a long-running hot-and-cold relationship with King Henry. The chef did admit to poisoning but said it was just a joke! That he thought he had put laxatives in the food. Although it was never proven that he was guilty of actually using real poison, it was the 1500s, so he was boiled alive on April 5, 1531. King Henry VIII apparently roared and cheered to the crowds, "I cooked the cook!"

THE BOATS

This method is also known as scaphism, an execution practice dating back to ancient Persia. The victim was put in between a pair of narrow row boats with their head, hands, and feet sticking out. This seems pretty mild . . . they even got to ingest large amounts of milk and honey. Honey was also rubbed all over the victim's face, hands, and feet, but still, that doesn't seem bad. Then the victim is set out to float on a river or lake. The honey stuck to them attracted hungry critters, and that sweet concoction of milk and honey is now causing them to diarrhea uncontrollably . . . in their boat. They are meant to sit in their shit, float, and be eaten alive. No rules on how long death would take, it could be days or weeks! Most victims died of dehydration, starvation, or septic shock.

KEEL HAULING

Since we're talking about boats, let's look at keel hauling! This execution method was practiced in the seventeenth and eighteenth centuries, primarily by pirates and the Royal Navy. It, too, involves boats and water but in a maybe more brutal way than scaphism? *Keel hauling* is Dutch for "to drag along the keel." What is a keel? We didn't know, either, but apparently it is the piece of material at the bottom of a boat that is integral to its structure. It runs longitudinally along the bottom center, and it's popular with the barnacles. Those sharp babies like to grow all over it! Victims were tied to the mast of the ship (the tall center thing) with rope and weights tied to their legs. Then, they were thrown into the ocean and dragged through the water. Because of the weights tied to their legs and the speed of the boat driving through water, the victim sank to the keel of the ship. There they would be sliced and diced by barnacles. This would last a few minutes, and then they would be pulled back onto the boat, given a moment to gather themselves, and thrown in again for more rounds of excruciating torture. Sometimes, victims would come up without their limbs . . . including their head! This would go on, the dunking and dragging, until they were dead.

The fucking Vikings, man. . . . They were gnarly. This execution is the worst of them all:

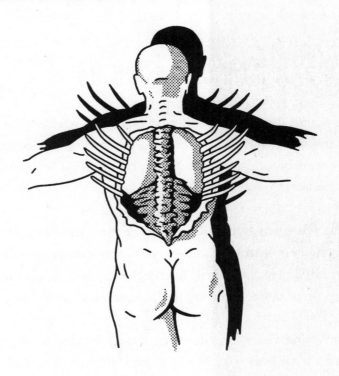

THE BLOOD EAGLE

The name alone gives us the ick. To begin, the victim is laid on their belly naked and likely tied down. As they lay there, an executioner drives a large knife or ax vertically across and through the victim's back, severing his ribs. The ribs are then pulled up and out of their back to give the look of wings. Wings! Then, his lungs are pulled up and out of his back, pulled across the ribs protruding from his back. It is unknown how long it would take a person to die during this process. They would most likely survive the pulling out and severing of the ribs but once their lungs are on their back, I mean we can't imagine long after that. Gruesome.

INFAMOUS LAST MEALS

Most people don't have the luxury of knowing what their last meal might be. But luckily for unlucky criminals, they get to plan ahead before, well, losing theirs. Here's a few particularly memorable stories . . .

Aileen Wuornos, probably one of the most infamous female serial killers in history, was executed for her crimes on October 9, 2002. Her last meal? She declined, instead opting for a nice cup of coffee. Fair enough, I mean sure, why not?

John Wayne Gacy, on the other hand, decided to take advantage. On May 10, 1994, the pedophile killer clown chowed down on a bucket of original-recipe chicken from KFC, a side of fries, and a pound of fresh strawberries.

Ted Bundy, like Aileen, declined a last meal before his electrifying execution on January 24, 1989, and was given a breakfast platter that included steak, eggs, hash browns, and a cup of coffee . . . but he didn't eat any of it. Wow, wasteful.

Philip Workman, who was executed in May 2007 actually had a very sweet sentiment, instead of a last meal he asked for a vegetarian pizza to be donated to homeless people in the area. The prison refused—which, like, come on, fuck off—but luckily members of the community caught wind and tons of pizzas were delivered to local shelters on his behalf.

If you thought John Wayne Gacy was gluttonous, **Lawrence Russell Brewer,** who was executed on September 21, 2011, was actually responsible for ending the whole last-meal request system due to his over-the-top demands:

- two chicken-fried steaks with gravy and sliced onions
- a triple-patty bacon cheeseburger
- a cheese omelet with ground beef, tomatoes, onions, bell peppers and jalapeños
- a bowl of fried okra with ketchup
- one pound of barbecued meat with half a loaf of white bread
- three fajitas
- a meat-lover's pizza
- one pint of Blue Bell Ice Cream
- a slab of peanut-butter fudge with crushed peanuts
- three root beers

And guess what, he didn't eat a damn bite. When it came time to feast, he said: "I'm not hungry." BYE.

And then we get to our favorite: **Thomas Grasso** asked for two dozen steamed clams and mussels, barbecue spare ribs, half of a pumpkin pie with whipped cream and strawberries, a double cheeseburger from Burger King, and a room-temperature can of SpaghettiOs. He was not having it when they gave him spaghetti instead of SpaghettiOs and his last words were "I did not get my SpaghettiOs I got spaghetti. I want the press to know this."

We've put great thought into this, and here's what we would want for our last meal:

Spencer
- fries and ranch (please no crinkle-cut)
- Neapolitan classic pizza
- a Diet Coke—but like a good fountain-soda Diet Coke
- chocolate chip cookie

Madison
- french onion soup
- fries and ranch
- wedge salad
- one (or five) margaritas
- banana cream pie and French toast

Hey, reader, on this note let's take a snack break, yeah?

OBITUARY

MARIANNE THERESA JOHNSON-REDDICK

Often when reading obits that rip someone to shreds, we feel a tinge of guilt because—is it really fair? In the case of Marianne Theresa Johnson-Reddick, it sure as hell is. Her adult children held nothing back when telling the world about the "violence, cruelty, and shame" their mother subjected them to. When the *Reno Gazette-Journal* published the obituary on September 13, 2013, it caused quite the international stir. Siblings Patrick and Katherine Reddick even went on a press tour to defend their mother's scathing obituary, explaining she beat and abused them and their siblings while running a brothel out of their Reno, Nevada, home. It was reported that Patrick Reddick sang, "Ding Dong the Witch Is Dead" when he found out his mother had died.

Marianne Theresa Johnson-Reddick born Jan 4, 1935 and died alone on Aug. 30, 2013.

Oh shit, that sentence alone tells us where this is headed.

Marianne's family continued on with the harsh facts: *She is survived by her 6 of 8 children whom she spent her lifetime torturing in every way possible. While she neglected and abused her small children, she refused to allow anyone else to care or show compassion towards them. When they became adults she stalked and tortured anyone they dared to love. Everyone she met, adult or child was tortured by her cruelty and exposure to violence, criminal activity, vulgarity, and hatred of the gentle or kind human spirit.*

Oh yeah . . . this one definitely puts the *bitch* in "obituary."

The obituary ends on a somber yet "packed with a punch" vibe:

Most of us have found peace in helping those who have been exposed to child abuse and hope this message of her death can revive our message that abusing children is unforgivable, shameless, and should not be tolerated in a "humane society." Our greatest wish now, is to stimulate a national movement that mandates a purposeful and dedicated war against child abuse in the United States of America.

Well there you have it!

9

IF THESE DOLLS COULD SPEAK

History has introduced us to some creepy AF dolls. The Mannenji Temple in Iwamizawa, Japan, houses the Okiku doll, which is known for its hair that reportedly grows over time. According to the legend, the doll was originally purchased by a young boy named Eikichi Suzuki in 1918. The doll, named Okiku, was a traditional Japanese doll with black hair and a kimono. Eikichi's sister, Okiku, loved the doll, and they played together every day. However, Okiku passed away at a young age, and after her death, the doll took over her spirit, causing its hair to grow.

During the late nineteenth century right here in the United States, there were popular tiny dolls made of porcelain or bisque called Frozen Charlotte dolls. The dolls were in rigid positions, lacking movable limbs. The story goes that the dolls were named after a girl named Charlotte, who in the 1800s wasn't properly dressed for a ball and froze to death in the carriage en route. A poem was even created for the Frozen Charlottes, warning young girls of the dangers of vanity and not listening to their parents. Bundle up, kids! But even these figures couldn't hold an embalmed candle to the real shit we'll get into next.

LA PASCUALITA

In March 1930, a beautiful mannequin graced the storefront windows of a wedding dress shop in Chihuahua, Mexico, called La Popular. The mannequin was beautiful, or should we say *is* beautiful, because it's still there to this day. The mannequin is very lifelike, with realistic skin color and texture, real hair, even wrinkles and veins on her hands and her legs! She has a super realistic-looking face, and her eyes even have makeup on. Pascualita is dressed in a beautiful wedding gown. She almost looks like a really good wax figure.

Now, when she arrived, the doll caused kind of an uproar in town as the locals started becoming very suspicious of this mannequin, as you don't see mannequins like this in storefronts. The story goes that the original shop owner, Pascuala Esparza, had a daughter who passed away tragically on her wedding day from a black widow bite. Apparently, the mother was in such deep mourning and grief that she had her daughter's body mummified and preserved, and that the mannequin is her real actual daughter. Customers have claimed the girl's eyes followed them while they were shopping or passing by. Others have mentioned she would suddenly change position! There is a pretty big resemblance between the mannequin and the real daughter, and it seriously makes us wonder: Is this really an extremely well-preserved woman from the 1930s or is it a great-looking mannequin? Either way, it's pretty incredible. Apparently, the mother has denied this, but nobody believed her. And, well, we would deny it, too.

The current owner of the store, Mario Gonzalez, does what he can to keep this legend alive. He still has the doll displayed in the window, and twice a week, he, or a few trusted employees, changes her dress. He only changes her behind curtains to preserve her modesty.

GRAVE DOLLS

Victorians knew how to mourn, honey. None of that printed pamphlet from FedEx kind of commemoration, these people were committed to going all kinds of extra for the deceased. Grave dolls, also known as mourning dolls or funeral dolls, were often made as a way to remember and honor a deceased loved one, particularly a child.

The history of grave dolls dates back to the eighteenth and nineteenth centuries when mourning rituals were a whole thing and extended periods of mourning were common. During this time, the death of a child was far more common, due to things like cholera, scarlet fever, smallpox, and typhoid. A lot of these diseases left people disfigured or in pretty bad shape, and embalming wasn't like it is today. Grave dolls were the answer to have something, dare we say—cuter?—to remember those who had passed. They were handmade by using a variety of materials, including cloth, porcelain, or wax. So, basically they started out as a typical doll. What classified them as funeral dolls was the fact they were often dressed in the clothing of the deceased and sometimes adorned with personal items such as locks of hair or other sentimental objects. These dolls were meant to look like the deceased child and were created with flat backs so they could comfortably sit propped up in a coffin during the funeral or burial ceremony. The dolls were used for the service and then kept as a memento or reminder of the dearly departed.

We feel kind of bad classifying these dolls as creepy

because they were truly meant to provide comfort to grieving parents who just wanted to maintain a physical connection to their loved ones. It has been said that many parents kept their mourning dolls in the child's crib, which toes our creeper barometer just over the line. There were also times when grave dolls were created to commemorate deceased adults, and we don't feel as terrible calling those creepy because, well, they are.

ASIAN DEATH DOLLS

The memorial practice of bride-doll marriage became popular in Japan during World War II. Basically, because so many young men were dying at the time without ever getting the opportunity to get married or have children, it was believed that this was considered a "bad death." In order to flip a bad death to a good one, it only made sense to marry these dead dudes off, regardless of being postmortem.

It wasn't just the missing out on marital bliss that made the living do this, people believed that the spirits of these dead single men would be restless and return to haunt their families. So, a solution was offered. They could simply have a posthumous wedding ceremony between the deceased man and a doll. Of course! They would do this by placing a photo of the young man and one of these bride-dolls in a box together, and it was thought that the "spirit bride" would then accompany the dead person for thirty years, until the deceased finally reaches the other world.

If one couldn't get a hold of a doll, no worries, there's always the alternate route many have taken throughout history . . . you could simply steal the corpse of a young girl! This is a practice that has continued *to this day*. In March 2013, four men in northern China were sentenced to prison for exhuming the corpses of ten women and selling them as ghost brides to the families of deceased, unmarried men. The women's bodies were to be buried alongside the dead men, ensuring eternal companionship.

Guess the saying is true: romance . . . is dead.

ONCE UPON A CRIME

Previously we've gone over body snatching, grave robbers, necrophilia, grave dolls, and this story involves all of the above.

Anatoly Moskvin was born in Soviet Russia in 1966. His fascination with cemeteries began at a very early age. As a young schoolboy, he would wander through the local cemeteries, specifically the Krasnaya Etna Cemetery located in the Leninsky District.

He later wrote about his childhood for a website called Necrologies, about an incident that happened when he was thirteen years old that really started his obsession with the macabre. On March 4, 1979, Anatoly was walking home from school when he encountered a funeral procession. This group of men in black suits stopped him on the street and forced him over to view the body of eleven-year-old Natasha Petrova, which you can imagine would be traumatizing enough. Well, they seemed to get a kick out of it for whatever reason, and the cruel men then forced him to kiss her on the mouth. He wrote, "I kissed her once, then again, then again." If that's not horrifying enough, the girl's grieving mother came over, put a wedding ring on Anatoly's finger, and another ring on her deceased daughter's, as if it was a marriage ceremony of sorts. Afterward they gave him a basket of fruit and sent him on his way. Holy horror.

Needless to say, this was very traumatizing, and led Anatoly down a very, very, very bizarre path in life. His obsession with death blossomed. He spent a lot of time studying the different gravestones at the cemeteries. He said after the bizarre marriage ritual with Natasha he felt this strange magnetism to cemeteries.

He managed to make his way through high school, eventually graduating from Moscow State University, where he vigorously studied Celtic history and folklore, learning thirteen different languages in the process.

It only furthered his interest in the occult and death, and to be honest, we think he would've loved our podcast *OBITCHUARY*. In his free time he would write about these topics, and his work was published many times. He didn't have any sense of a social life, and is said to have been somewhat of a recluse. Any time he left the house, it was usually to peruse the cemeteries. He said he visited a total of 752 between 2005 and 2007 and had taken detailed notes on each of the graves. He would write down the names of the deceased, their dates of birth and death, and scour the obituaries to find their stories.

He eventually started sleeping at the cemeteries, on one occasion sleeping in the casket of a person scheduled for burial the following day. But it wasn't because he was tired. In his college studies he had learned that the ancient Druids slept on graves in order to communicate with spirits of their dead. He also studied the culture of the peoples of Siberia, where he discovered they had a similar practice for communicating with the dead. This led him down a path where he had his sights on finding the graves of children. He would look up their obituary to figure out what had happened to them, and if he felt connected to them, he'd go sleep on top of where they were buried.

Had it stopped there, we might just be like, "Hey, that's kinda crazy, Anatoly," but it didn't stop there. In fact, it got a whole lot crazier. Anatoly wanted to be physically closer to the deaths he was researching, so he started digging, and sleeping with even more bodies.

Life at home was pretty tame for Anatoly. He abstained from drinking, smoking, drugs, and sex, and lived with his parents in a two-bedroom apartment. They had to know something was off, right? Like *Oh, good morning, Anatoly, you're covered in dirt and smell like shit— where were you all night?*

He was barely making any money from his writing career, and when he was home, he confined himself to his room. He did have a girlfriend at one point, and they actually tried to adopt a child together because he didn't want to have sex, but their application was denied because of his low income. He reportedly never had sex with that girlfriend. Totally shocking news, Anatoly was a virgin.

Cut to 2009, locals were beginning to discover that the graves of their loved ones were being desecrated; some of them had been completely dug up. They started complaining. Local officials were concerned enough to hire security companies to monitor the cemeteries. Without any leads, the problem continued for the next two years.

On November 2, 2011, forty-five-year-old virgin Anatoly was caught by police messing around with some of the tombstones at the local cemetery. Eight police officers jumped at the opportunity to apprehend him because they were thinking he must be the guy. They launched an immediate investigation and decided to visit the apartment where he lived with his parents to see if they could collect any evidence.

When they got there, they inspected his bedroom, and inside were just piles of books and tons of dolls.

But as they began investigating these dolls closer, they realized that they were not dolls at all. They were the mummified remains of deceased children who had been dug up from various cemeteries over the course of ten years.

Later we'd come to find out Anatoly believed that he might be able to magically bring the children back to life one day. He thought maybe if they were more comfortable at home with him, their spirits would openly communicate with him.

In total they found twenty-six bodies. He turned them into dolls by drying them out using a combination of salt and baking soda. He thought their remains would be too decayed and ugly for them to be happy once they came back to life, naturally, so he did his best to prevent the natural process by wrapping the limbs in strips of cloth and stuffing the body cavity with rags and padding. He sometimes added wax masks over the faces before dressing them in colorful children's clothes and wigs. And get this, he inserted buttons or toy eyes into the girls' eye sockets so they could watch cartoons. With all this work done, the bodies appeared to be large homemade dolls, which concealed them for what they were. His mother even said she thought it was his hobby to make such big dolls and didn't think anything strange of it. Okaaay.

Anatoly confessed to forty-four counts of abusing graves and dead bodies. He said to the victims' parents, "You abandoned your girls, I brought them home and warmed them up." They had him undergo a psychiatric evaluation to see if he was fit to stand trial, and surprise, surprise, he was not. On May 25, 2012, he was deemed unfit to stand trial after he was diagnosed with paranoid schizophrenia during the evaluation, and ended up being sent to a psychiatric clinic for some much needed help, and that is where he remains to this day.

Anatoly allegedly told authorities to not bother reburying the girls too deeply, as he will simply un-bury them when he is released.

OBITUARY

CHAN HOLCOMBE

What's more horrifying? Getting circumcised by your dad's pocket knife or having your family tell the world you were circumcised by your dad's pocket knife? Asking for a friend, Chan Holcombe, whose family put him and his penis on blast in his obituary posted on Dignity Memorial in October 2011. When we first read this seemingly typical article it was like, nice guy from Arkansas, respected veteran, loved to fish—*record scratch*, they said what? So many questions. *Chan Holcombe, 72 of Fort*

Smith passed away Thursday, October 13, 2011. He was born July 14, 1939 in a Log Cabin in Bates, AR to the late Ralph and Inez Holcombe and was circumcised with his Dad's pocket knife. He loved to fish and caught a lot of crappie. He was an Air Force Veteran, a member of the Disabled American Veterans, and an Entrepreneur.

PART 4

TILL DEATH DO US PART
(AND MAYBE NOT EVEN THEN)

10

LOVE REMAINS

We all know that classic wedding phrase "till death do us part." It's like the grand finale of wedding vows, and it's been around for ages. The very idea of two lovebirds, promising to stick together through thick and thin, in sickness and in health, until the grim reaper shows up with his cloak and scythe. Yep, that's the deal. It's like saying, *We're in this for the long haul, and not even death can tear us apart.* But the fact is, death does—at least on a physical level—tear us apart. And for many of those deep in love, they refuse to accept that as their fate. They vowed to stay together, and dammit, that's what they'll do: dead or alive.

COMPANION PLOTS (DOUBLE BURIALS)

Now, there are different types of plots you can buy at the cemetery. There are your single plots, probably the most common type of plot. It's your basic grave plot for one. A studio, if you will. Then, there are family plots, which are actually really sweet but, we heard things can get complicated when there are spouses, an asshole uncle, and so on. And then there are companion plots. These types of burial plots are typically for a couple. They consist of two plots together or one big plot for two. The couple is either buried side by side or one on top of the other.

This got us wondering, can two pals or lovers share a casket for their eternal slumber? First off, the rules for this cozy arrangement can vary depending on where you die (legally speaking, of course). Then there's the size of the casket—you can't squeeze two sumo wrestlers into a phone booth, right? But the most important part is what the dearly departed and their family want. If they're super tight, like peanut butter and jelly, some states might say, "Sure, why not?" Especially if they're a married duo or as close as family can get. But in most places, sharing a casket is a hard no.

So, here's the deal—if you and your forever love would like to cozy up in a coffin for eternity, you'd better plan ahead, making sure everyone's on board with the plan and budget for customizing one of these double-wides.

And with that, we'll tell you some stories about how romance really is dead, beautiful stories of lovers who took forever beyond the grave.

THE LOVERS OF MODENA

This story takes us to Italy in 2009, where a pair of skeletons was unearthed by archaeologists. Now, you might think they stumbled upon a war cemetery, but it was more like dirt and a few plots. These skeletons, dating back to the fourth or fifth century CE, held a secret that would make them famous— they were buried side by side, holding hands!

Two adult males, likely in their twenties, resting peacefully for centuries, hand in hand. It's enough to make you say, "Aww!" But the mystery deepens. Were they really lovers, or could they have been close comrades or perhaps even family members who met a tragic fate on the battlefield?

We can't say for sure whether they were romantically involved or not. Who knows? But one thing is for sure—they were close till the end.

In any case, it's a heartwarming sight to imagine these two souls finding solace in each other, even in the afterlife. And hey, if they were fully homosexual and got dubbed as lovers, well, that's just another layer to this sweet, ancient mystery. Love knows no boundaries, even in the annals of history!

VALDARO LOVERS

Again, in the enchanting land of Italy, a couple years before the Lovers of Modena, archaeologists stumbled upon another astonishing sight—a pair of ancient male and female skeletons locked in an eternal embrace. They lay facing each other, in a cozy fetal position, their limbs intertwined, and love radiating from their very bones. These two lovers, not a day older than nineteen or twenty, are an astounding six thousand years old!

But that's not all; there's a twist to this ancient romance, too. Alongside them, buried in the earth's cradle, were two flint knives, a flint blade, and an arrowhead. Now, you might think, "Did they meet a violent end?" But no, there were no signs of a tragic demise.

Many believe that this young couple, frozen in time and each other's arms, may have been caught in the unforgiving embrace of a cold Italian night, desperately seeking warmth. However, archaeologists have theorized that they were actually placed in this tender position after their passing, a testament to the deep connection they shared in life.

Archaeologists, showing the utmost respect for this eternal bond, chose not to disturb the lovers. Instead, they carefully transported the entire slab of earth that cradled them, ensuring that their ancient love story remained undisturbed, locked in a forever embrace. It's a tale that reminds us that love, even across millennia, knows no boundaries or limits.

EMBRACING SKELETONS OF ALEPOTRYPA

Deep within the heart of a cave in Greece, archaeologists once again stumbled upon a pair of skeletons locked in a tender embrace, just like two lovebirds spooning. These star-crossed lovers, believed to be in their early twenties, hailed from different sexes, one male and one female. They've been spooning for roughly 5,800 years, a testament to the enduring power of their love. And a testament to the everlasting love of the spoon.

Now, here's where it gets intriguing. Unlike some other cases, archaeologists don't believe that these lovers were arranged in their intimate position after death. Instead, it seems that they naturally found solace in each other's arms, even in their final moments.

The mystery deepens when it comes to the cause of their passing. Although it's unclear how they met their fate, anemia was a prevalent cause of death in that region during their time. Still, the exact circumstances remain shrouded in history's enigmatic embrace.

HASANLU LOVERS

In 1973, an intrepid archaeological team unearthed a pair of skeletons in an ancient Iranian city, revealing a story that's more than 2,800 years old!

These star-crossed lovers met their end around 800 BCE, and their bones held a profound secret. No evidence of injury or disease was found, leading experts to believe they perished from a more insidious foe—asphyxiation. It's likely they were seeking refuge, hiding from invading forces or seeking shelter from the choking smoke of fires set by those very invaders.

But what makes this story truly enchanting is their eternal embrace. Picture this: Skeleton One lies on their back, arm tenderly draped around Skeleton Two. Skeleton Two, on their side, appears to rest their hand gently on Skeleton One's face. It's a tableau of love frozen in time, like a romantic bedtime scene where Skeleton Two leans in for a loving kiss.

As for their identities, Skeleton One is believed to be a male in his early twenties, while Skeleton Two, originally thought to be female, has sparked debate. Some experts now suggest that Skeleton Two might also be male.

AUNT EASTER AND UNCLE SOG

This tale combines love, devotion, and an unusual burial that left a lasting impression on those who witnessed it.

Our story takes us back to the 1930s, where Aunt Easter Johnson Eubanks and Uncle Sog Eubanks lived a life intertwined with love and family. This devoted couple had around ten children, making their home a bustling hub of activity.

But on one fateful day, October 15, 1937, tragedy struck when Aunt Easter succumbed to a lingering illness and passed away at home. Her husband, Uncle Sog, couldn't bear to be without her and turned to prayer, fervently praying for his own demise.

Remarkably, Uncle Sog's prayers seemed to be answered, for just a few hours later, he too departed from this world. The news of their passing reached the local coffin maker, George, who had a talented helper named Tommy.

Tommy had a bold idea—why not create a double coffin for this inseparable couple? George, after some contemplation, agreed that it was a brilliant notion. With great care and craftsmanship, they constructed the double casket, a unique final resting place for Easter and Sog.

However, the article from the *Madison County Musings* suggests that the preparation of Uncle Sog's body was not without its challenges, as the person tasked with shaving him needed several stiff drinks to gather the courage. Nevertheless, the frail form of Easter, weighing no more than eighty pounds, and the tall, slender frame of Sog found their place together in the double coffin, right in front of their home.

Photographs were taken to document this unusual but

touching moment. Eldorado Eubanks, one of Sog's brothers, stood behind the double casket in one of the pictures.

The love and devotion shared by Easter and Sog left a profound mark on the community, and their united burial in the double casket became a cherished memory for all who attended the simple ceremony at Groseclos Cemetery, south of Japton. Today, their resting place is marked by a double stone, adorned with a glass-encased picture of Easter and Sog, overlooking the serene Lollars Creek Valley in Madison County. It's a testament to a love that defied even the boundaries of mortality.

RAYMOND AND VELVA BREUER

The Breuers were a couple who left this world hand in hand in 2017 after an incredible seventy-seven years of marriage!

Raymond and Velva's love story began in their childhood, where they attended the same one-room schoolhouse. In a twist of fate, young Raymond made quite the impression on Velva by jabbing her with a hot poker from the school's fireplace, leaving behind a scar. As the story goes, Raymond once quipped that Velva married him to get even for that fiery encounter.

But their love was undeniable. They celebrated seventy-seven years of marriage, and at their anniversary party, Velva expressed, "I wouldn't trade him for anybody. He's so good."

When their time came, Raymond passed away at the age of ninety-seven, with Velva by his side, holding his hand until the very end. Overwhelmed by grief and declaring that she couldn't go on without him, Velva followed her beloved husband just thirty hours later.

Their children, deeply touched by their parents' inseparable bond, made a poignant decision—they chose to lay Raymond and Velva to rest together, in the same coffin. They approached the funeral director, and with a willing heart, their wish was granted. What a beautiful way to honor a love so profound that not even death could separate them.

LUCIA AND EMMA GUARA

Double burials aren't solely reserved for couples. In 2021, a different story unfolded, one involving two sisters who found their eternal rest side by side. Love and family, it seems, can inspire unique final arrangements that speak to the enduring bonds of human connection. In a heartbreaking tale filled with unimaginable loss, we remember Lucia and Emma Guara, two young sisters whose lives were tragically cut short in the Surfside, Florida, condo collapse.

Lucia, at the tender age of ten, and little Emma, just four years old, were taken from this world far too soon. Their parents, too, did not survive the devastating collapse, leaving behind a void that words can scarcely describe.

In their final journey, these inseparable sisters found solace in each other's company. They were laid to rest side by side in a beautiful white coffin, a touching tribute to the unbreakable bond they shared in life and in their untimely passing. It's a poignant reminder of the love that will forever connect them, even in eternity.

HEART BURIALS

During the medieval times, heart burials were all the rage. But wait, what exactly is a heart burial? Well, it's exactly what it sounds like—the heart is lovingly removed from the deceased's body and given its own special resting place, separate from the rest of the remains. Literally—a heart burial.

But here's the twist—it wasn't just the heart that got this VIP treatment. Nope, sometimes, folks decided to take it a step further and bury a person's guts along with their heart! Why, you ask? Well, back in those days, when people passed away far from their hometowns, transporting an entire body was not only logistically challenging but also a surefire way to invite a host of unsavory infections.

You see, organs and intestines are like the sprinters of decomposition—they break down the fastest. So, to ensure a safer and more practical journey back home, your dearly departed's heart and guts might just be making a separate trip. It's a curious historical practice that sheds light on the creative ways our ancestors dealt with the challenges of their time.

Don't believe us? Check this out:

KING HENRY I OF ENGLAND

This unfortunate soul met his end in quite an unusual manner—by indulging in a jawless fish that didn't quite agree with his stomach. Food poisoning struck, and alas, he never recovered.

Upon his demise, he received the honor of embalming at the Rouen Cathedral, a practice reserved for the elite and noble. But here's where things get truly fascinating.

First, his heart and intestines were carefully removed and found their resting place at the priory of Notre-Dame-du-Pré. But that's not all—even his brain and eyes were taken out! By this time, the body had begun to emit a rather unpleasant odor, so they resorted to scented balm to mask it. To prevent decomposition, his flesh was rubbed with salt and then wrapped in ox hides.

Now, here's the (even more) bizarre twist: the poor soul tasked with removing Henry's brain met a rather unfortunate end himself due to the overpowering stench! *(Enter sounds of us gagging.)*

The journey of Henry's corpse to England hit some un-expected delays, thanks to a fierce winter gale that grounded the ship in Caen for four long weeks. Despite all precautions, black fluid began to seep from the ox hides, a grim reminder of the mortal coil's impermanence.

Finally, at Christmas, a favorable wind graced their sails, and the ship, accompanied by a solemn escort of monks from Saint-Étienne, set sail for England. Henry's body found its final resting place at Reading Abbey, while his brain, tongue, eyes, bowels, and even his heart, remained interred at the cathedral in Rouen.

RICHARD THE LIONHEART

Dashing Richard the Lionheart was a king with both a lion's courage and a heart full of chivalry. This king of England, from 1189 to 1199, was not just known for his rugged hand-someness but also for his fierce determination. Born as the son of King Henry II, he had quite the complicated relation-ship with his father. It seems he was quite the mama's boy, and together with his mother, they hatched plots against his father.

Things got so intense that Richard even campaigned against his own dad in France. And guess what? He won! King Henry II had to surrender to his own son. Bold move, kid.

Richard's reign was marked by bravery and battles. He was always at the forefront, leading his troops to victory in numerous conflicts. However, his remarkable life came to a rather unfortunate end when he was struck by a crossbow bolt, right in the shoulder. Tragically, the wound turned gangrenous, and Richard, the fearless warrior, had finally met his match.

On his deathbed, Richard, despite being in pain, summoned the person who had shot him. This young man sought revenge against Richard, claiming that Richard had killed his two brothers and his father. You might expect vengeance to be the order of the day, but no. Richard, in a display of remarkable forgiveness, not only spared the young man's life but also gave him one hundred shillings and set him free.

As for his remains, Richard's heart found its resting place at Rouen in Normandy; his entrails in Châlus, where he met his end, and the rest of his body was buried at the feet of his father at Fontevraud Abbey in Anjou.

Intriguingly, a scientific analysis of Richard's heart in 2012 revealed that it had been embalmed with various substances, including frankincense, symbolically important because it had been present both at the birth and embalming of Christ.

THOMAS HARDY

Hardy, an English poet and writer, born in 1840, lived through the Victorian era, although he was quite critical of it. In 1874, he married Emma Gifford, and they shared their lives until her passing in 1912. In 1927, Hardy fell ill with pleurisy, an inflammation around the lungs and chest. On his deathbed, he penned his final poem, dedicated to his beloved wife.

Thomas Hardy had a heartfelt wish to be buried in

Stinsford, Dorset, England, alongside his late wife. He even expressed a desire to share the same grave. However, at the time of his death, his estate was valued at nearly seven million, and his executor had other plans. The compromise reached was that his heart would be buried with his wife in Stinsford, and his cremated body would find its resting place at Poets' Corner in Westminster Abbey.

PERCY SHELLEY

Percy Shelley, husband of the brilliant mind behind *Frankenstein*, Mary Shelley, has quite a tale as well. He was an English poet known for his romantic poems and an interest in the occult. Shelley was also an atheist, which drew its fair share of criticism.

Percy and Mary Shelley shared a profound connection, and it's said that they first exchanged their "I love yous" at her mother's grave. In 1822, Percy faced a dramatic end when his boat, the *Don Juan*, was sunk in a storm. After a ten-day search, his badly decomposed body washed ashore. A few weeks later, he was cremated, but the story doesn't end there.

His heart, it seems, had other plans. Despite the cremation, Percy Shelley's heart would not burn due to the calcification caused by tuberculosis earlier in his life. Mary and friends witnessed the heart's resilience during the cremation on a beach.

Then came the heart's curious journey. Mary wanted it as a keepsake, but a friend of Percy's took possession and initially resisted giving it to her. Eventually, the heart found its way to Mary, who carefully wrapped it in silk and stored it in her writing desk. While some historians debate whether it was truly a heart or perhaps a liver, let's embrace the romantic notion that it was indeed his heart, a symbol of love that transcended even death.

DEATH BY BROKEN HEART

This one goes out to all the lovers in the audience tonight, as we're answering a question that's been asked throughout history: Can you die of a broken heart? Turns out yes, you can.

It's called broken heart syndrome, a.k.a. takotsubo cardiomyopathy, and according to the American Heart Association, it's a reaction your heart has to a surge of stress hormones caused by an emotionally stressful event. Throughout our research, over and over again we kept seeing that the condition was caused by extreme stress or intense emotions, but we also read on the Mayo Clinic's website that it can actually be caused by a serious physical illness or surgery as well.

The Mayo Clinic goes on to say: "People with broken heart syndrome may have sudden chest pain or think they're having a heart attack." Only part of the heart is affected by broken heart syndrome, which temporarily disrupts the heart's usual pumping function. The rest of the heart continues to work properly or may even squeeze (contract) more forcefully.

It essentially works a lot like a heart attack, in fact the two main symptoms mirror heart attacks completely: chest pain and shortness of breath. The difference is that typical heart attacks are generally caused by a complete or near complete blockage of a heart artery. In broken heart syndrome, the heart arteries are not blocked, although blood flow in the arteries of the heart may be reduced.

Now let's get into the nitty-gritty, how and why does this happen? Is it because you lost the love of your life and you simply can't function without them? Sometimes. It is still a bit of a mystery.

Let's also talk about the name takotsubo cardiomyopathy. *Takotsubo* is actually a Japanese word for "octopus trap," because when you look at the heart while someone is suffering an attack, it looks like an octopus trap. We've seen the videos on YouTube, and we have to agree on this one.

Johnny Cash, the legendary country singer-songwriter, passed away on September 12, 2003, just four months after his beloved wife, June Carter Cash, died on May 15, 2003. June was not only Johnny's wife but also his musical partner and a significant influence on his life and career. They had a deep and enduring love that was well documented.

While it's common to say that someone died of a "broken heart" when they pass away shortly after the loss of a loved one, it's usually not a medical diagnosis in the traditional sense. In Johnny Cash's case, it's more accurate to say that he experienced profound grief and health problems in the wake of his wife's death. June's passing deeply affected him, and he struggled with his health and emotions.

Johnny Cash had a history of health issues, including diabetes and a long battle with substance abuse. His health had been declining for several years before his death, and he was hospitalized for various complications. It's likely that the combination of these factors contributed to his passing.

While it's difficult to pinpoint a single cause of death in such cases, it's clear that Johnny Cash's grief over losing June played a role in his declining health. His love for her was undeniable, and her loss had a significant impact on him. So, while we can't say he died of a broken heart in a medical sense, it's evident that her death had a profound emotional and physical toll on him in his final months.

Mary Tamm, known for her role as Romana in *Doctor Who*, was a beloved actress, especially among fans of the show in the United Kingdom.

Tragically, Mary Tamm passed away in 2012 due to cancer, leaving behind her husband, Marcus Ringrose. It's not uncommon for loved ones to feel a profound sense of loss and grief after the death of a spouse, and this was clearly the case for Marcus.

After delivering the eulogy at his wife's funeral, Marcus was in the process of writing thank-you notes to those who had sent condolences, likely trying to cope with the loss and express gratitude for the support he and his family had received. It was during this difficult moment that he passed away from a heart attack.

Thomas and John Lamb, a real heart-wrencher. In the summer of 2015, Thomas Lamb, a father, lost his life in a brutal attack involving a pitchfork, all stemming from a dispute over a game of pool. This horrifying incident occurred right outside his home in Edinburgh, Scotland.

What makes this tragedy even crazier is the fact that Thomas's sixty-seven-year-old father, John Lamb, was inside their shared home, completely unaware of the violent events unfolding just outside until after his son's death. The loss of his beloved son was an immense burden for John to bear, and he was still grappling with the grief when he, too, passed away, only eleven weeks after the tragic loss of his son.

Doug Flutie, a former NFL quarterback, had his parents pass away within minutes of each other. Flutie's father was in the hospital after suffering a heart attack and eventually succumbed to the damage his heart had taken. Less than an hour later, his mother, no doubt devastated from the loss, also suffered a heart attack and died.

Debbie Reynolds's death in 2016, just one day after the death of her daughter, Carrie Fisher, led many to speculate that she died of a broken heart or the emotional stress of losing her child. Reynolds expressed an understandable profound grief over the loss of her daughter, and her health had reportedly been in decline in the months leading up to her death. It's possible that the emotional stress and grief played a role in her overall health, but it's essential to recognize that determining a precise cause of death can be complex, especially when there are multiple contributing factors. In her case, the stroke was the primary cause listed on her death certificate, but we think most would agree it was likely connected to her broken heart.

OBITUARY

LINDA WEIDE

Robert Weide, the Emmy-winning director and executive producer of *Curb Your Enthusiasm* during its initial five years, wrote a heartfelt good-bye to his late wife, Linda, who passed away in December 2022. Weide's touching tribute was featured in the *Los Angeles Times* and paints a poignant picture of how Linda preferred to enjoy her time, emphasizing her unassuming and easygoing nature during their twenty-eight years together.

Linda Weide, my remarkable wife, believed everybody's age was no-body's business. Let's just say she was ageless and timeless. She had a kind of elegance from another era. She studied acting under Stella Adler, who told her, "My dear, you should only play queens." She was certainly my Queen for 28 years, 25 married. In 2018, she was diagnosed with Progressive Supranuclear Palsy, a rare but fatal neurological disease. (Please Google it.) Her bravery and dignity in the face of this illness were awe-inspiring. But unfortunately, the House always wins. She died on Christmas Day, 2022, peacefully, at home, and in my arms. If you must die, try to do it in the arms of someone who loves you. It helps.

She was born in Follansbee, West Virginia, to Lucy Gianinni and Victor Ubieta. Her Aunt Lee and Uncle Eli Rabb were important figures in her upbringing. She attended Bethany College, where she received a B.A. in Liberal Arts.

She lived for a time in Boston, then Manhattan. In 1989, she moved to Los Angeles. Thank G-d for that last move, because on September 30, 1994, I walked into Café Aroma in Studio City, and there she was. She had it all—beauty, style, grace, intelligence, wit, a great laugh, a blinding smile and (can I say this in 2023) legs that demanded to be shown off, and were. That night, I wrote in my journal, "I think I may be in big trouble." We were married on July 11, 1998.

She was remarkably low maintenance. We both appreciated the occasional meal in a fine restaurant and traveling abroad, but some years I'd ask what she wanted for her birthday, and she would answer, "a grilled cheese sandwich." Typical. She was generous to a fault, always putting others' needs before her own. Her softest spot was reserved for animals, especially those in need. Our own animals were all rescues, and friends would tell her, "If I can come back in another life, I want to be one of your animals." Her favorite charity was Best Friends Animal Sanctuary, but she donated to many others.

Understandably, she would become disenchanted with acting, but two memorable roles were that of "Penelope" in the 2001 L.A. stage revival of Kurt Vonnegut's "Happy Birthday, Wanda June" (she was asked to play the part by Vonnegut), and the role of "Mindy Reiser" in the "Curb Your Enthusiasm" episode, "The Terrorist Attack." She is also featured in the 2021 documentary "Kurt Vonnegut: Unstuck in Time," which is dedicated to her.

What a team we made. She was Gracie to my George. After we purchased side-by-side cemetery plots years ago, I asked her what she wanted her marker to say. She answered, "I'm with Stupid." (That request will not be honored.) Oh, dear—what am I ever supposed to do without her.

They say, "Nothing lasts forever," but they didn't know about my love for her. 28 years wasn't nearly long enough. Still, I may just be the luckiest SOB who ever lived. Rest well, Bunnie. I hope we'll be together again.

For those who never knew her, I'm sorry for your loss.

11

PET CEMETERIES: WHERE OUR FURRY FRIENDS REST IN PEACE

We all adore our pets—our four-legged companions who bring endless joy to our lives. But, let's face it, thinking about their end-of-life journey is downright heart-wrenching. The idea of parting with our beloved pets is a thought we often shove into the furthest corners of our minds until it becomes a reality.

The dilemma arises—what do we do when our pets pass away? Do we give them a proper burial, opt for cremation, or perhaps even taxidermy? Of all the choices life throws at us, pet afterlife arrangements might just be the trickiest. But fear not, because in this pet-friendly adventure, we're diving into the enchanting world of pet cemeteries.

A BRIEF HISTORY OF PET CEMETERIES

Pet cemeteries and pet burials have a history that stretches back tens of thousands of years. Historically speaking, people have been loving on their fur babies for a long, long time.

ASHKELON'S ANCIENT DOGS

Ashkelon National Park in Israel, a treasure trove of history, witnessed an astonishing discovery. In the years between 1986 and 1994, a canine mystery arose. What they found were 1,300 dog skeletons, each resting in its own individual shallow grave. Remarkably, these furry companions seemed to have met their natural ends, showing no signs of fatal injuries or violence. Their peaceful repose raises intriguing questions about the beliefs and customs of ancient times.

Various theories abound, with some speculating that these dogs were laid to rest due to epidemics that swept through the land. Alternatively, it's posited that the ancients attributed special healing properties to a dog's saliva, turning these faithful friends into revered figures in their society.

KOSTER SITE

In the quiet town of Eldred, Illinois, history lies beneath the soil, where the oldest cemetery in eastern North America is located. Dating back to ancient times, this cemetery boasts more than three acres of history, spanning from the Early Archaic period around 7500 BCE to the Mississippian period around 1000 CE. But what truly sets it apart are the remarkable remains of domesticated dogs, interred more than eight millennia ago.

The graves are humble and unmarked. Yet, in their silent repose, they tell a profound story. The absence of elaborate markers suggests a simplicity that speaks to the hearts of those who laid them to rest. Here, the dogs were not forgotten but were buried alongside adults and children, revealing the deep and lasting bond between humans and their four-legged friends in times long gone by.

SHAMANKA II AND THEIR
BELOVED DOGS

At Russia's Lake Baikal, the passage of time reveals a heart-warming connection between humans and their loyal companions, even seven thousand years ago. At the Shamanka II site, the remains of a dog bear witness to a profound bond. In death, this beloved canine received more than just a burial; it received a heartfelt farewell.

Alongside the dog's resting form lay treasures of deep significance—a meticulously carved antler spoon, a necklace adorned with the teeth of red deer. These precious items spoke volumes about the affection these ancient humans held for their best dog friends.

Archaeologist Robert Losey summed it up beautifully: "To them, it was a member of the family. It had a soul."

BERENICE'S ANCIENT ANIMAL
COMPANIONS

In Berenice, Egypt, archaeologists unearthed the remains of more than six hundred animals, a diverse array that included dogs, cats, and even monkeys. What sets this find apart from the ordinary, however, is the evident tenderness with which these animals were laid to rest.

Unlike previous discoveries of mass animal graves, these creatures were not sacrifices or objects of veneration. Instead, they were cherished, beloved pets. Adorned with collars and bearing signs of gentle care during their twilight years or times of ailment, these animals tell a story of genuine affection between humans and their loyal companions.

These cemetery sites remind us that our connection with animals goes back thousands of years. The bond between humans and their pets, whether in life or after, is truly remarkable.

Pet cemeteries are far from being a thing of the past; they're very much a part of our present. Today, people continue to honor their fur friends with a proper final resting place, keeping the tradition alive and well. So, if you're ever in need of a heartwarming reminder that not everyone sucks, pay a visit to one of these modern pet cemeteries, where love for our four-legged companions lives on.

MODERN PET CEMETERIES

HYDE PARK, LONDON

In 1536, Hyde Park served as King Henry VIII's hunting ground. However, by 1881, its role evolved when a family sought permission from the park's gatekeeper to lay their beloved dog, Cherry, to rest there. Their request was granted, and Cherry's small tombstone still stands as a testament to this unique tradition. Over time, more pet lovers followed suit, and by 1903, Hyde Park had transformed into an official pet cemetery, with approximately three hundred furry companions resting in peace. Today, visitors can explore this special corner of the park, located in the far northwest.

THE CEMETERY OF DOGS AND OTHER
DOMESTIC ANIMALS, PARIS

In 1898, France decided that pets deserved more than to be
discarded like yesterday's leftovers, and thus, the Cimetière
des Chiens et Autres Animaux Domestiques was established
in Asnières, a suburb of Paris. Officially opening its gates in
1899, this unique cemetery owed its existence to Marguerite
Durand, a journalist and the founder of the newspaper *La
Fronde*, who had a rather unconventional pet herself—a lion
named Tiger. Fast-forward to 1987, and this pet cemetery
became a historical monument, falling under the city's care.
With its lush trees, exquisite statues, and opulent gravestones,
this cemetery is a true masterpiece. Upon entry, you're
greeted by Barry, a heroic Swiss rescue dog credited with sav-
ing forty lives. Well, it's a statue of him; his actual body was
taxidermied and returned to Bern. Today, it serves as the final
resting place for approximately four thousand pets, including
cats, dogs, fish, chickens, hens, monkeys, and even horses. It
even boasts the resting place of the silent film star Rin
Tin Tin.

HARTSDALE CANINE CEMETERY

Hartsdale Canine Cemetery, nestled in Hartsdale, New York,
has quite the history. Founded by none other than Sam-
uel Johnson, a compassionate veterinarian instrumental in
establishing the ASPCA, this cemetery is a testament to his
unwavering dedication to our pets. It's a fitting tribute to
the man who helped shape the way we care for and honor
our pets.

These are even more remarkable pet cemeteries that deserve a brief mention. The Los Angeles Pet Memorial Park in Calabasas, California, is home to memorials for some unique animals, including the iconic MGM lion, Tawny. On the US Naval Base in Guam, you'll find the National War Dog Cemetery, which honors twenty-five military dogs that bravely served during the Second Battle of Guam in 1944. Over in Presidio, California, the Presidio Pet Cemetery boasts 424 animal graves, tucked away in a charming neighborhood, surrounded by a protective white picket fence. We couldn't leave out the Reveille Mascot Cemetery, the final resting place for pooches who have served as mascot for Texas A&M. The graves sit outside of the football stadium, with a perfect view of a scoreboard so the dogs can know the score, even in the afterlife. And, of course, who could forget Disneyland's Haunted Mansion Pet Cemetery? While fictional, the cemetery features memorable characters like Big Jake, Penny the elephant, Stripey and Lilac the skunks, Bully the frog, Fifi the poodle, Rosie the pig, Old Fly Bait the frog, Long-Legged Jeb the spider, Freddie the bat, Kai the koi fish, and a few unnamed animals, making it a whimsical homage to our cherished animal companions.

GRIEVING ANIMALS

We've talked a bunch on our podcast about different grieving practices in humans, but taking a peek into the world of animal grief was mind-blowing. Grief after the loss of a loved one is just like an innate thing, right? It's something everybody deals with, this sense of remorse or anguish over the death of a loved one. Animals are no different. They, too, experience grief, and throughout the different species they have their own individual ways of dealing with death. Scientist Marc Bekoff has done a ton of research on emotional reactions within different species and has reported that grief has been seen in wolves, chimpanzees, magpies, elephants, dolphins, otters, geese, sea lions, and many more.

A lot of researchers have studied the emotions of chimpanzees, likely because they possess so many human-like qualities. Dating back to 1879, a man named Arthur E. Brown did a case study on a chimpanzee who lost his female counterpart and noted that the male subject cried in a way that its keeper claimed he had never heard. This chimpanzee also showed symptoms of depression, although he seemed to bounce back after a few days.

Which is something we kind of noticed when researching; it seems like grief in animals is more short-lived than the human experience. While we're on the subject of chimps, Jane Goodall, a very famous expert primatologist and anthropologist, noted that a chimpanzee named Flint, who lost his friend Flo, also displayed signs of grief. She said, "He walked along one of the branches, then stopped, and stood motionless, staring down at an empty nest." Flint had been lethargic, refusing food, hollow-eyed, gaunt, and utterly depressed. A *Smithsonian* article talks about another instance, where a small group of captive chimpanzees was carefully observed after one of their members, an elderly female named Pansy, died. The chimpanzees checked Pansy's body for signs of life and cleaned bits of straw from her fur. They refused to go to the place where Pansy had died for several days afterward.

In somewhat recent years, there was a really famous case of animal grief. In 2018, an orca whale carried the corpse of her dead calf for more than two weeks. Scientists called it "the tour of grief." The adult female, named Tahlequah, who is known as J35 by scientists, was seen after her tour swimming without the body of her calf. "J35 frolicked past my window today with other J pod whales, and she looks vigorous and healthy," Ken Balcomb, founding director of the Center for Whale Research, wrote in an email to the *Seattle Times*. The twenty-year-old orca moved people around the world who were touched by her mourning after she gave birth on July 24. The four-hundred-pound calf that was born that morning, which was the first live birth in the pod since 2015, lived only about half an hour. Scientists believe she had previously lost two other offspring since 2010. The most recent death "may have been emotionally hard on her," Balcomb said.

Although scientists often scoff at the way people love to anthropomorphize animals, in this case researchers said that the whale's actions were what they looked like: mourning. "You cannot interpret it any other way," Deborah Giles, a killer whale biologist at the University of Washington, told the *Washington Post*. "This is an animal that is grieving for its dead baby, and she doesn't want to let it go. She's not ready." Scientists called the grieving period unprecedented for a southern resident killer whale, noting that while it wasn't uncommon for dead babies to get carried around for part of a day, it never went on that long.

There are many scientists who kind of look down on this research around animal grief behavior because they think as a society we tend to humanize animals more than we should, but to them we say fuck off—the proof is in the pudding.

Elephants exhibit profound patterns of grief. They've been observed standing guard over a stillborn baby for days, their heads and ears hanging low in mourning. Orphaned elephants, having witnessed their mothers' tragic deaths, have been known to wake up from nightmares screaming. Elephants even have a communal way of acknowledging a deceased relative, much like they do when welcoming a newborn. They gather around the lifeless body or old bones, possibly wailing in their unique way, and collectively touch them.

In 2016, doctoral students in Africa captured a remarkable elephant grieving ritual on video. Members from three different elephant families came together to pay their respects to a deceased matriarch. They engaged in an emotional display of smelling, touching, and repeatedly passing by the corpse. It's a fascinating sight, and as the *National Geographic* narrator explains, elephants have glands behind their eyes that stream when they experience heightened emotions, akin to crying, whether from happiness or profound sadness.

Animals, with their incredible capacity for emotion, display various forms of grief that are both heart-wrenching and fascinating. Sea lion mothers, for instance, emit eerie squeals when they witness their babies being consumed by killer whales. Dolphin mothers, even after their calves have passed away, exhibit signs of grief and try to save them, eventually coming to terms with their loss.

Geese, too, share in this experience of mourning. Zoologist Konrad Lorenz once observed that when a fellow goose died, the others would have their eyes sink deep into their sockets, and they'd display an overall drooping demeanor, as if the weight of loss bore down upon them.

And then there are the magpies, whose behavior is truly astonishing. These birds engage in what can only be described as magpie funerals. They bury their dead under twigs and grass, showcasing a remarkable understanding of mortality.

And crows, known for their intelligence, have been found to respond to the loss of one of their own with organized gatherings. These avian assemblies, akin to little mobs, involve intense squawking, an expression of their collective sorrow.

In essence, the animal kingdom's capacity for grief is undeniable. Despite the scientific community using different terminology, the raw, innate emotion of grief is abundantly evident in the animal world, reminding us of the deep connections we share with these remarkable creatures.

CADAVER DOGS

One subject that really gets us going is working dogs, and no, this isn't going to be another tearjerker. We're talking about cadaver dogs and some incredible search and rescue pups.

Cadaver dogs are dog detectives trained to pick up the scent of human remains, hence their other name, human-remains-detection dogs. They might seem similar to search and rescue dogs, but their job is quite distinct. While the latter sniff out the general scent of humans, cadaver dogs specialize in the delicate art of detecting decomposing flesh. These incredible canines are 95 percent effective at picking up the scent of human decomposition, even from bodies buried up to fifteen feet deep.

Law enforcement agencies rely on these remarkable dogs to help solve crimes where a deceased person is involved. Not only do they provide valuable evidence for the courtroom, but they also offer closure in cases where missing persons are assumed to be deceased but not yet confirmed. Often, cadaver dogs team up with search and rescue dogs to find both living and deceased humans.

Now, what makes these trained cadaver dogs so astonishingly effective? It's all about those noses! While we humans boast a modest six million olfactory receptors in our noses, a dog takes the gold with a whopping three hundred million. Their sense of smell is roughly forty times better than ours. They've got incredible sniffers that can do things ours can't even dream of. They can breathe and smell at the same time, thanks to the nifty separation of their air passage. And here's the kicker—each nostril can smell things separately, kind of like how we see in 3D.

But how does one become a trained cadaver dog? In an interview with BuzzFeed News, cadaver dog trainer Jason Purgason, who runs Highland Canine Training in North Carolina and has more than twenty-five years of experience, spilled the kibble on the process. He doesn't discriminate based on a dog's sex or breed; instead, he looks for qualities like drive, a dog's ability to hunt persistently, and how they handle different environments. Age does matter, though. Training is most effective with dogs aged one to two and a half years old, but it's not impossible with older pups. Once Purgason has a candidate, he and his team use actual human remains to train them. Think hair, teeth, bones, tissue, and blood. Yep, the real deal. Getting your paws on these isn't easy, and no, he's not into grave robbing (he clarified this with a chuckle). There are products like ScentLogix that offer chemical training aids and even full-on cadaver detection kits. These kits cover every stage of decomposition and can also help train dogs in explosive detection, drug detection, electronics, and even biological infestations like mold and bedbugs. Pretty impressive!

Cadaver dogs are like canine detectives, and they come in three different flavors, as expertly explained by Jason Purgason, the seasoned cadaver dog trainer:

Field cadaver dogs: These are the fur-coated detectives that search for human cadavers in a variety of locations. Whether it's dense forests, vast fields, or even cars and homes, they're on the case.

Disaster cadaver dogs: When disaster strikes, these dogs shift from rescue to recovery mode. They're the brave pups who scour disaster areas, be it the aftermath of natural calamities or man-made tragedies. You might remember their heroic presence during the recovery operations after 9/11.

Water cadaver dogs: These aquatic experts can locate the scent of decomposition underwater. Yes, you heard that right! They're the ones who can dive into rivers, lakes, and other watery spots to find remains. Curious how they manage it? During decomposition, a body releases gases that rise to the surface. These gas cues can be picked up by these skilled dogs, guiding officials to bodies underwater.

A moment of respect for some specific dog heroes:

The Bavarian Ripper, also known as Andreas Bichel, terrorized early nineteenth-century Bavaria with his gruesome murders. For those intrigued by this dark chapter, a cult literature deep dive might unveil more chilling details. Two women mysteriously disappeared in 1806 and 1808, with Bichel suspected of involvement. During the investigation, authorities discovered clothing from these women in his home, though not enough for an arrest. A fortunate twist of fate occurred when a court clerk, walking **Court Clerk Dog** past Bichel's house, noticed the canine's persistent interest in a woodshed. What they found inside was horrifying—a woman's body, cut in half. This gruesome discovery led to further investigations, Bichel's confession, and his subsequent arrest.

Now, let's pivot from this unsettling tale to a brighter one about **Pearl**, the pioneering cadaver dog. Pearl, a yellow Lab, joined the scene in 1974 with the New York State Police. Her training was formal, and her skills quickly proved invaluable.

Within a year, she helped locate the body of a college student who had been brutally murdered and buried four feet deep. A true canine hero.

Apollo, a German shepherd, entered the spotlight during the harrowing aftermath of 9/11. A seasoned search and rescue dog, Apollo was nine years old at the time of the attack. He wasted no time and began searching for victims just fifteen minutes after the second tower fell. Although he's not credited with finding anyone that day, his unwavering determination stood out. He had to be pulled away from the search, as he simply wouldn't stop. At one point, he fell into a hole and emerged covered in debris but miraculously unharmed due to having been soaked while navigating through the water at Ground Zero. Apollo's incredible efforts earned him the prestigious Dickin Medal, a testament to his heroism.

The aftermath of 9/11 saw several search and rescue dogs and cadaver dogs in action. Among them were **Roselle and Salty**, both Labrador retrievers and guide dogs for the blind. They received the Dickin Medal as well for guiding their owners and numerous others to safety from the World Trade Center's collapsing towers. Salty refused to leave his owner's side, guiding both out of the building, and Roselle led her owner and thirty others to safety during the chaotic evacuation.

Twist and Trimble, two cadaver dogs, played a crucial role in the Laci Peterson murder case. Twist was sent to the Petersons' home and Scott Peterson's warehouse, consistently leading her handler to a bathroom in the warehouse, where it turned out the crime had been committed. Meanwhile, Trimble guided her handler to a location near the end of a pier at Berkeley Marina. Tragically, Laci's body was discovered in San Francisco Bay.

Lastly, **Buster**, a black Labrador retriever, made headlines in 2013. His owner, retired detective Paul Dostie, reached out to Steve Hodel, the son of George Hodel, a suspect in the Black Dahlia case. Buster was given permission to sniff out George Hodel's famous Frank Lloyd Wright–designed house, where he stopped at various spots in the basement, on the front steps, and at the back of the property. It's believed he detected the scent of old blood. Buster's remarkable skills also took him around the world, where he located unmarked graves and recovered the remains of missing servicemen.

AN HOMAGE TO A TRUE HOLLYWOOD STARLET

This obituary by Patty Lane was published by CNN back in 2009 and warmed our hearts to say the least.

Uttering the words "Yo Quiero Taco Bell," Gidget, a female dog, played a male dog in the commercials.

Take that, gender norms! The obituary went on to add some more insight into how this came to be.

She was cast as the girlfriend of the Taco Bell Chihuahua, but the di-

rector changed his mind at the last minute and made Gidget the lead dog, [trainer Sue] Chipperton said.

Honey, she had the it factor!

"She was kind of typecast, so she never really got much work after that," Chipperton said.

The "laid back" and "happy" starlet had roles in *Legally Blonde 2* and *Beverly Hills Chihuahua.*

"That's what her life had come to over the years," playing small background roles, Chipperton said. The Chihuahua loved being on set. She *"acted like a big dog and had a big dog attitude,"* Chipperton said, adding that once she arrived on a soundstage, she had no trouble finding her way in front of the camera.

The penned memorial ended with:

"It's comforting," she said. *"It's so touching to see so many people were affected by her and that they loved her, she was a very special dog."*

12

KEEP IN TOUCH

DEATH PHOTOGRAPHY

Death photography, also known as postmortem photography or mourning photography, was a practice that became popular in the nineteenth century. It involved taking photographs of deceased individuals, often in a posed and lifelike manner, shortly after their death. These photographs were usually commissioned by the deceased person's family as a way to remember and mourn their loved ones.

There were several reasons for the popularity of death photography during this time:

High mortality rates: In the nineteenth century, especially in the early part of the century, death rates, particularly among infants and young children, were high due to diseases and lack of medical advancements. As a result, death was a lot more normalized than it is now. People seemed to have been more practical when it came to death and looked at it as another part of life, one that also deserved to be commemorated.

Lack of other portraits: For many people, especially those in rural or less affluent areas, having a photograph taken while alive was a rare and expensive luxury. A postmortem photograph might be the only image a family had of their loved one.

Mourning and memory: These photographs served as a way for families to remember the deceased and to aid in the grieving process. They could be displayed in the home and shared with friends and relatives.

Death photographs were usually taken with great care to present the deceased in a peaceful and lifelike pose. Sometimes, props were used to make the person appear more alive, such as open books or eyes held open with devices. In the case of infants, they might be posed in cribs or with their toys.

During the nineteenth and twentieth centuries, the Victorians had a unique relationship with death. Rapid urbanization and industrialization brought pollution and overcrowding to cities, combined with a lack of knowledge about hygiene in a pre–germ theory society. This resulted in the rampant spread of diseases like scarlet fever, typhoid, tuberculosis, diphtheria, and cholera, which were often fatal. Infant and child mortality rates were shockingly high, with some areas in London recording a staggering 33 percent death rate for children under five in 1849.

For adults, life wasn't much rosier. While those who reached adulthood had a chance at relatively old age, the average life expectancy at birth was dismal. In 1850, it was just forty years for men and forty-two for women. These figures are a far cry from today's worldwide average life span of approximately seventy-one years, thanks to modern medicine and improved living standards.

Postmortem photography during this era was a formal and thoughtful process. Great care and sensitivity were invested in every aspect, from the attire the deceased were dressed in to the choice of setting for the photograph. All of this had to be done while dealing with the less pleasant physical aspects of a deceased body, including decomposition, rigor mortis, and the glassy-eyed stare that often accompanies death.

In some instances, makeup or paint was applied to the deceased's face to conceal the telltale signs of death, like sunken eyes, pallid skin, and a lifeless expression. For example, a touch of rouge might be used to create the illusion of flushed cheeks. Skilled artists even painted open eyes over closed eyelids to give the appearance of wakefulness.

The photos themselves can be undeniably eerie. Due to the limitations of old cameras, subjects had to remain perfectly still during long exposure times. This meant that the deceased person in the photograph often appears very clear and lifelike. In contrast, any slight movement by the living individuals around them could result in a blurry, ghostlike figure. These ghostly apparitions are a hallmark of photographs from this era.

It's worth debunking a common myth here. Contrary to what you might read on the internet, very few deceased individuals were propped up in standing positions for photographs. In fact, it was nearly impossible. Early photography required long exposure times, and there's no way a posing stand could have supported the weight of an adult corpse, let alone in a dignified and lifelike posture. Additionally, rigor mortis, which sets in two to six hours after death and can last up to eighty-four hours, makes posing a body incredibly challenging. So, while postmortem photographs may seem spooky, they're a fascinating reflection of a bygone era's approach to death and memory.

As photography technology improved and became more accessible, death photography gradually declined in the late nineteenth and early twentieth centuries. It became more common to have photographs taken while the person was still alive. However, this practice remains a fascinating part of photographic history, providing a glimpse into how people of the past dealt with mortality and remembrance.

One of our favorite topics is Victorian spirit photography, a peculiar photographic practice that gained popularity during the Victorian era in the late nineteenth century. It involved creating photographs that purportedly captured images of ghosts, spirits, or other supernatural phenomena alongside living subjects.

Here's how it typically worked:

Double exposure: The most common technique involves double exposure. The photographer would take two separate exposures on the same photographic plate or negative. The first exposure would be of the living subject, while the second would be an image of a ghostly figure or some other spooky element. Since the plate wasn't developed between exposures, both images would appear on the final photograph.

Superimposition: Another technique was superimposing two different negatives during the printing process. This could be done using a variety of methods, including careful blocking or masking during printing.

Reflections and props: Photographers sometimes used mirrors, hidden wires, and props to create ghostly or supernatural effects. For example, a mirror could reflect a hidden person or object, making it appear as though they were part of the scene.

Spirit forms: Some photographers claimed to capture spirit forms or ectoplasm on film. These were often wispy, fog-like shapes that would surround or hover near the living subject; this again is a result of double exposure and other camera tricks.

Spirit photography was especially popular during a period when spiritualism, a belief in communicating with the dead, gained a following. People were intrigued by the idea of using photography to provide evidence of life after death.

Notably, spirit photography was controversial even during its heyday. Many believed it was a form of fraud, and some photographers were exposed for manipulating images to deceive their clients. Famous spirit photographers like William H. Mumler and William Hope faced legal challenges related to their work.

William H. Mumler was a fascinating guy. His story is a significant part of the history of spirit photography. In the 1850s and 1860s, he was working as a jewelry silver engraver in Boston. Photography was a hobby for him, and he dabbled in it when he had spare time.

One day, on October 5, 1861, Mumler decided to take a self-portrait, something like a modern selfie. During that era, achieving a clear image required long exposure times, often a minute or more. So, he would set up the camera, take the photograph, dash into the frame, stand still for a minute, and then check the result.

To his astonishment, when he examined the developed photograph, it wasn't just him in the picture. Alongside him, standing near a table and chairs, was a woman dressed in white. What made this even more extraordinary was that the woman resembled his deceased cousin, who had passed away twelve years earlier.

Mumler believed that he had accidentally captured a spirit, specifically the spirit of his deceased cousin, on film. This incident sparked his interest in spirit photography, and he began taking more photographs, claiming to capture images of departed loved ones alongside the living. His work gained fame, and he started offering his services to others, helping them connect with their deceased family members through his photographs.

While he initially regarded his accidental photograph of a "spirit" as a joke, news of his image spread rapidly. During the Victorian era, a time marked by both a fascination with death and spiritualism and the backdrop of the American Civil War with its significant loss of life, Mumler's newfound skill found a receptive audience.

Ironically, Mumler himself was not a spiritualist; he did not share the beliefs of those who sought to communicate with the deceased. However, this seemed to work in his favor. He played up the narrative that he was as astonished as his clients by his supposed ability to channel the spirits of departed loved ones.

Mumler made a pivotal career shift, leaving his job as a jewelry silver engraver to become a full-time photographer. He worked in a studio owned by Hannah, a woman who was not only a photographer but also a medium. This union between photography and spiritualism seemed almost fated, and the two married shortly thereafter. Hannah was even known for designing mourning hair wreaths, further tying her to the Victorian obsession with death and remembrance.

People flocked to Mumler's studio for spirit photographs, willing to pay a significant sum for a chance to connect with their deceased relatives. His fees, which could reach up to $10 (equivalent to around $357 today), didn't deter eager clients. However, his work also faced skepticism and accusations of fraud. Many believed that he manipulated the images or collaborated with people who posed as spirits. In fact, he even faced a highly publicized trial in 1869 but was ultimately acquitted.

Whether one views Mumler's work as a clever hoax or a means for people to find solace in troubled times, his story remains a remarkable part of the Victorian era's complex relationship with life, death, and the afterlife.

William Hope's journey into the realm of spirit photography shares similarities with William Mumler's. In 1905, as an English carpenter with a penchant for photography, Hope was merely experimenting with his camera when something extraordinary happened. While taking a photo of a friend, an unexpected presence appeared in the image: apparently the spirit of his friend's deceased sister.

This experience spurred Hope to delve deeper into spiritualism. He founded the Crewe Circle, a spiritualist group, and assumed a leadership role within it. The Crewe Circle grew in size and influence, even garnering support from renowned figures like the author of the Sherlock Holmes series, Sir Arthur Conan Doyle. Skepticism surrounded Hope's work, but it was an era marked by significant grief, particularly due to World War I. Many people sought solace and connection with their departed loved ones, opening themselves to such phenomena.

Unlike Mumler, Hope faced several exposures of his methods. In 1920, a man named Edward Bush, under a false name, sent Hope a photo of his deceased son and later sat for a spirit photograph. The twist was that the picture Bush mailed was of a living person, yet the spirit of his supposed deceased son appeared in the photograph, complete with the fake last name Bush had provided.

However, the most significant exposure of Hope occurred in February 1922 when Harry Price, one of history's most famous ghost hunters, investigated him. Price, known for debunking various paranormal phenomena, was sent by the Society for Psychical Research to scrutinize Hope's work. In a clever move, Price secretly marked Hope's photographic plates. When the resulting photographs lacked these marks, it was clear that Hope had switched the plates to produce spirit images.

Remarkably, even after being exposed as a fraud, Hope maintained a substantial following and continued his spirit photography until his death in 1933.

BURIAL KEEPSAKES!

Burial keepsakes have always fascinated us. What would you want to be buried with? Let's take a look at some intriguing stories of people and the unique items they were interred with, from largest to smallest.

ARCH WEST

This man is a hero for Dorito lovers everywhere. He was the creator of Doritos and served as the marketing vice president at Frito-Lay. When he passed away in 2011 at the age of ninety-seven, he was buried with a sprinkle of Doritos. Attendees at his funeral were even given Doritos to toss into his grave, adding a quirky and fitting touch to his final resting place. Love this guy!

HUMPHREY BOGART

The legendary actor, known for classics like *Casablanca*, had expressed a desire to be cremated and have his ashes scattered at sea from his boat. However, in the 1950s, cremation was still relatively uncommon in the United States. Despite his intentions, Bogart's remains were cremated and interred at the Forest Lawn Memorial Park in Glendale, California. Accompanying his remains was a gold whistle, once part of a charm bracelet he had given to his wife, Lauren Bacall. Their love story began on the set of *To Have and Have Not*, where Bacall's character famously uttered the line, "You know how to whistle, don't you, Steve? You just put your lips together and blow." The whistle bore a sweet inscription: "If you need anything, just whistle."

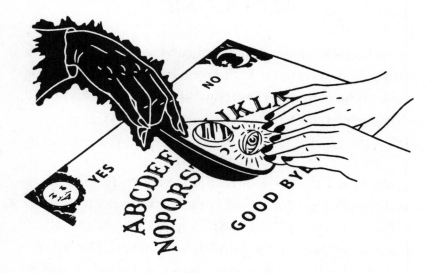

HARRY HOUDINI

The great escape artist and magician had a close bond with his mother. In his last will and testament, Houdini specified that his coffin must include a pillow made from stacks of letters he had received from his late mother over the years. Interestingly, after his mother's death, Houdini turned to spiritualism in an attempt to communicate with her. However, his efforts were in vain, leading him to become a prominent skeptic of mediums and séances. He dedicated himself to debunking these practices, famously stating, "It takes a flimflammer to catch a flimflammer."

BELA LUGOSI

Known for his iconic portrayal of Count Dracula in the 1931 film, Bela Lugosi was buried in his Dracula costume, complete with his cape. It was a fitting tribute to the role that made him a legend in the horror genre.

ROALD DAHL

The beloved author of children's classics like *Charlie and the Chocolate Factory* and *Matilda* had a unique send-off. When he passed away in 1990, he was buried with his favorite pencils, wine, chocolates, a pool stick, and even a power saw, making for an eclectic assortment of keepsakes for the afterlife.

FUNERAL FAVORS

While we're on the topic of keepsakes, have you ever thought about funeral favors? Giving attendees a physical memento that encapsulates their deceased loved one is a common practice. Were they known for a specific recipe? Why not send mourners home with a personalized recipe card from their collection. Was the dearly departed known to have a green thumb? A little succulent could serve as a sweet reminder.

The memorial for Spencer's mother, Laurel, was held at the Claremont Hotel in the Berkeley Hills. It was a classic setting to celebrate a classy woman. The support was overwhelming, a true testament to her character, four hundred people flooded in to offer their condolences. I, Spencer, stood away from the entrance outside near the valet stand. It was too much to handle. My best friend, Carolyn, sat with me as I chain-smoked cigarettes; it was then an old high school friend of my mom's saw me from the corner of her eye. She let out an animalistic scream. It scared me at first, but I couldn't help but crack a smile, looking at my friend Carolyn very much in a *Are you seeing this?* way.

The friend in question wailed, "Spencer, can you please help me find my way inside?"

"No," I responded. It might sound harsh, but here I am, twenty-seven years old, deep in my grief, about to lay my mother to rest. She vanished shortly after without a word. If there's one thing I took from losing my mother, it was learning to put my needs first. The day was emotional, tense, loving, somber. A whirlwind. As a token of our appreciation and as a way to have a physical reminder of our mom, we handed out flower seed packets: "Laurel's Florals." I guess you'd call it a funeral favor. If memory serves me right, we also had little baskets of my mom's favorite gummy bears set out for the taking.

In the days that followed, we received so much support from our friends and extended family. The texts piled in, and then my sister and I started receiving messages about the "beautiful rocks." What the hell were these people talking about? "I put my rock in my kitchen window so I can think of your mom every day!" "My rock is in my garden with the flower seeds."

I asked my sister: "What the fuck are they talking about? What rocks?!"

Well, turns out that her whacky friend who'd bombarded me prior to the service had written my mother's name in red Sharpie on rocks you would see in somebody's driveway.

It was one of the few times my sister and I just looked at each other and were able to lose it in laughter instead of tears during those dreary days.

Did we want guests walking around thinking that we wrote our mother's name on rocks typically utilized to weigh down newspapers? Absolutely not, my mother would've been aghast, but I will never be more grateful for that tiny fit of laughter during a time I wasn't sure I'd ever laugh again.

Long story short; don't hand out favors at a funeral without permission. And just know that no matter how fucking hard life is, you'll eventually laugh again.

GALVANIC REANIMATION

Oh, the things you'll come across when you google things like what they used to do to cadavers! (Name something more sus than our search history. Seriously.)

It all started with two guys named Luigi Galvani and

Giovanni Aldini, and their curious observations of frogs' legs twitching when touched with a scalpel. Galvani took things a step further by incorporating electrical currents, which led him to believe in the concept of "animal electricity." This phenomenon was due to electrical currents stimulating the fluid connecting the nerves.

Giovanni Aldini, Galvani's nephew, took these experiments further. He began experimenting on animals with more complex nervous systems, such as pigs, sheep, cows, and oxen. The electrical currents made their eyeballs roll and tongues move, which piqued his interest in the potential to reverse death. Yep, you read that right.

Aldini eventually progressed to experimenting on cadavers, often obtained from executions. However, he encountered challenges with bodies that had been beheaded, as the lack of blood and fluids limited their response to electrical stimulation.

In London, Aldini obtained the body of George Foster, who had a grim history of drowning his wife and children. In a public display, Aldini attached probes to Foster's cadaver and left them for a few hours. Although he didn't succeed in resurrecting the deceased, the experiment did produce some eerie effects. The jaw quivered, facial movements occurred, and one eye even opened. This public experiment contributed to the legend surrounding Aldini, inspiring Mary Shelley's portrayal of Dr. Frankenstein.

Giovanni Aldini took his experiments on the road, conducting public demonstrations for a fee, which drew curious crowds eager to witness these electrifying experiments.

On a related note, Dr. Guillaume-Benjamin-Amand Duchenne, often referred to as "Dr. Smile," made significant contributions to the understanding of facial expressions and how they relate to the use of electricity in the 1800s. Duchenne's work involved mapping out the facial muscles responsible for different expressions. By applying electrical stimulation to specific muscles on a corpse, he aimed to decode facial expressions and correlate them with mental states. His experiments were documented through photography, providing valuable insights into the science of facial expressions. These historical accounts not only are intriguing but also highlight the curious and sometimes macabre aspects of scientific exploration in the past.

ONCE UPON A CRIME

THE ACCIDENTAL CREMATION OF AURELIE TUCCILLO

We feel it's a pretty commonly known fact that after a body is embalmed, it's not a perfect resemblance of what the person actually looked like when they were alive. Hence why George Hamel didn't really think twice when he went for a final look at his sister, ninety-five-year-old Aurelie Tuccillo, at her wake.

But her son Ralph was even more suspicious. Was this a case botched by a mortician?

Whispers started throughout the service, and more and more family members began questioning Aurelie's appearance. And they had every

right to be suspicious . . . because the corpse indeed belonged to somebody else.

"A lot of people noticed, let's put it that way," the bereaved son said.
"The response I got was, 'No that's not her.'"

Apparently, Buckmiller Brothers Funeral Home, who at the time vehe-
mently denied the body wasn't Aurelie's, eventually admitted she had
accidentally been cremated, and they had placed another body that had
been set for cremation in her casket instead. IMAGINE.

EPILOGUE

Well, it's time to seal our coffin! We hope you enjoyed our little romp through death. Our aim was to make you laugh and teach you something new while maybe changing how you see death. It's a scary topic, one that is hard to comprehend, but learning about it gives us power. We wanted to show that it's okay to talk about it and that knowledge can help us understand it better.

In the end, death is the one thing that connects us all. It's a universal truth we'll all encounter. As time passes and new methods, funeral practices, and traditions emerge and change, we'll continue sharing and explaining them to you. But amid this evolution, we'll always cherish the incredible (and occasionally bizarre) history of customs surrounding death.

Exploring the chapters of human existence interwoven

with mortality's tale has been both enlightening and humbling for us. While we can't claim expertise on death, crafting this book has helped us shed some fear surrounding it. Along the way, we found ourselves laughing at the absurdities that shaped our modern approach to death. Our wish for you is to take action! Organize that will, sort out funeral arrangements, and express your affection to those you cherish. Because, truthfully, none of us knows when our time will come to an end. We wish that the farewell for you or your cherished one is a splendid one, brimming with everything that was meaningful and dear to you or them. Perhaps a themed funeral, an iron casket, or the warmth of a retort?

Most important, we hope that you feel confident in taking a little creative liberty when writing an obituary! As you read, we love a colorful one . . . but a scathing one really gets us going! Throw someone under the bus if you need to! Obituaries are expensive, so get ya money's worth!

As we bid farewell, may this hot book serve as a catalyst for reflection, appreciation, and perhaps a newfound perspective on the profound and intricate relationship between life and the ever-present shadow of death.

P.S.: If you somehow thought this was a self-help book on dealing with death—this is the epilogue, you're too late, babe! But, we'll leave you with this:

Dr. Colin Murray Parkes, psychiatrist and grief expert once said, "Where there is deep grief, there is great love." And we couldn't agree more.

ACKNOWLEDGMENTS

So many incredible people in our lives have helped us bring this book to fruition; first and foremost we'd like to thank our listeners without whom we'd be talking to ourselves in a room.

We'd like to thank our team at United Talent Agency, namely Dan Milaschewski, Lily Dolin, and Shelby Schenkman.

Allie Kingsley Baker for being our partner and showing us the ways of the writing world.

The entire team at Plume, including our superstar publisher Jill Schwartzman for being our guide.

The incredible illustrations by Lauren Griffin.

On a personal note we'd like to thank our friends and family for dealing with our chaotic schedules, supporting us while we fulfill our dreams.

Ash Cisek and Alaina Urquhart for bringing us onto the Morbid Network and supporting our creative endeavors.

Hotdog, Doris, and Desi for their constant companionship, and Francisco Reyes Jr. for putting up with us and designing our logo.

P.S.: We'd be fools not to acknowledge Swingers Diner in Los Angeles for being our late-night refuge after recording sessions and brainstorming. Oh and for the best ranch dressing.

About the Authors

Best friends and cohosts **Spencer Henry** (*Cult Liter Podcast*) and **Madison Reyes** have a long-running history of sending each other the wildest, most absurd, and sometimes scathing obituaries. In 2021, they decided to share their findings with the world when they launched *OBITCH-UARY*, the hilarious, hit weekly podcast, and it turned out the world was eager to hear it. Today, Spencer and Madison continue to podcast together and both live in Los Angeles when they're not touring the country to spread the *OBITCH-UARY* message.